EXPLORING SACRED SENSUALITY

A NEO-TANTRIC WORKBOOK

BY JES SHICK

DEDICATION

To my tantric mentor and guide,
Denise Greenfield.
May you rest in divine safety.

To all the teachers, clients, friends, and family
who have loved, supported,
and challenged me along the way.

And to my beloved best friend and life partner, Paul.
Thank you for always seeing me,
even when I couldn't see myself.

Table of Contents

Introduction

This workbook is born from a lifetime of spiritual seeking. From my first meditations for calming asthma attacks as a child, to beginner tarot readings and academic spiritual studies as a teen, I have been on a journey to understand the nature of reality and to use my findings to uncover a sense of peace, safety, and joy.

Along the way, I could see that sensuality is a powerful and enigmatic gateway to understanding and experiencing spiritual transcendence. In 2010 I stumbled across an ad online from a Tantra teacher who was looking for an apprentice. I learned from this goddess of a woman for many years. She taught me personally, she taught me professionally, she taught me through her workshops, and she taught me through her mistakes.

This work is the result of 14 years of offering private tantric guidance sessions. It is inspired by every client and couple who felt moved by our time together and asked me for something tangible to take home so that they wouldn't forget. Over all those years my practices have shifted and evolved in countless ways, but certain core techniques and concepts have remained consistent over the years. It is these foundational elements of sacred sensuality that have made their way into this workbook.

Sacred sensuality can be an elusive concept that means different things to different people. This is partly because the very idea of what is sacred can shift drastically from person to person. In fact, Tantra is not a lineage that asks you to renunciate your beliefs in order learn because it sees everything in existence as a manifestation of divine consciousness. This workbook is not here to tell you what is sacred, but to help you connect with your own version of deeper meaning, of the divine, and of personal spiritual empowerment.

What this workbook does suggest is that your body and your senses are key to understanding less obvious and more mystical layers of our reality. Rather than striving to do each practice perfectly, I invite you to turn your awareness inward and to celebrate each sensation as meaningful. I call for you to linger in moments of feeling so that you can experience the power of your own present awareness when it meets your body's natural energy. When combined with intention and breath, your senses and your pleasure can transform you.

If there was a stated goal to our time together in a session, it would be to help you FEEL the warm, breathy, connected space that is at the core of tantric practice. Because of this, a tantric ceremony can be very dreamlike. We walk through the unseen realms of the body until we uncover your sacred spark of divine awareness and evoke its power to help you heal and connect. In these pages, I hope to support you in feeling empowered to connect with that dreamy space and uncover your own divine spark.

A Note About Real Tantra

NEO-TANTRA VERSUS CLASSICAL TANTRA

Please understand that every concept and exercise in this workbook is the tip of an iceberg.

This creation comes at a time when the world is waking up to the pitfalls of cultural appropriation, a time when museums are beginning to repatriate much-loved artifacts to their countries of origin, when indigenous people are finally being recognized for their historic and cultural contributions to humanity. And that context gives me a framework for the tension I have felt as a tantric practitioner in the west.

I have to hold a paradox. I've been taught to share powerful practices of guidance, breathwork, meditation, touch, and sacred sensuality. These were given to me as "Tantra" and I accepted them into my heart and have shared them with folks for years, always feeling so honored and blessed that I get to create such a beautiful space with people.

As my education and practice have deepened, I have had to face the reality that this meaningful work is not what a native practitioner would call Tantra, and that there is a need to decolonize indigenous spiritual practices. Academics and practitioners alike have gracefully offered up the term "Neo-Tantra" to encompass the ways that the Western world has adapted Tantra to its own cultural context. I use this term to acknowledge that, as an American, I can lay no claim to the lineage of Tantra.

I have often considered dropping the word Tantra all together and instead refocusing on the concept of sacred sexuality, but that is where the paradox comes in. To reframe my practice away from Tantra is to unplug from the undeniable roots of my work. I have spent 14 years getting to know the teachings and finding ways to bring more concepts from Classical Tantra into my sessions and worldview. I land at a place of "yes/and"- True, what I am offering to you is not Classical Tantra AND it is also deeply inspired by it. So here I want to extend my deepest, most humble respects to the originators of these techniques.

I encourage and ask of you, not only to take some time to explore Classical Tantra, but also to see Neo-Tantra as more than a watered-down version of something more authentic. Let this be a gateway for you to dive deeper, not only into yourself, but also into a wider global context and history.

RESOURCES FOR CLASSICAL TANTRA

- Christopher D. Wallis
  - "Tantra Illuminated: The Philosophy, History, and Practice of Timeless Tradition"
  - www.tantrailluminated.org
- Swami Satyasangananda Saraswati
  - "Sri Vijnana Bhairava Tantra: The Ascent"
- Abhinava Gupta
  - "Tantraloka"
  - "Tantrasāra"
- Richard K Payne & Glen A. Hayes
  - "The Oxford Handbook of Tantric Studies"
- Dr. Mark Dyczkowski - www.anuttaratrikakula.org

How to Use this Workbook

THE WINDING PATH TO SENSUAL FULFILLMENT

You will find that this is not exclusively a sex manual nor is it a meditation manual that is devoid sexuality. Both this workbook and my practice address the whole spiritual self as a path to sensual fulfillment. As my professional path evolved over the years, I learned just how important it is for a person to understand and embody these foundational concepts before their true sensual nature can unfold. Though some of these practices may seem tangential to your sexuality, I invite you to take notice along the way of your shifting perception of pleasure and its roles in your life.

EXERCISES

The lessons and exercises in the beginning of this book are sequential based on the flow that I use in an introductory tantric guidance session. I recommend fully reading each exercise before trying it out. This does not mean that you have to do them in the order that I have laid out, but it may be supportive to do so. If you are well versed and experienced, then you also probably know how valuable it is to continually revisit these basic building blocks of your practice and learn from them in new ways.

On the next page, you will find a section titled Creating a Sacred Practice Space in Your Home that is designed to help you create a place in your world that can be a container for you to dive deep. Especially when you are just getting started, it can be hard to reach the depths of a meditation at a dining room table covered in mail or on a couch with a distracting tv nearby.

WRITTEN REFLECTIONS

Suggested writing reflections are included to help you remember your experience. Did you have a vision? A unique memory? A new sensory experience? Write it down because meditations and somatic experiences can be dreamlike or easy to forget. Ideally, this book is something you can come back to for years as a reminder of your journey.

SENSATION MAPPING

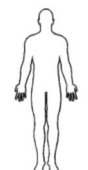

Where you see this symbol, you are invited to shade, sketch, or color the sensation you feel in your body. I encourage you to get creative! Consider how you can draw different sensations. Does heaviness look like black lines? Does sadness look like dark blue shading? Does pleasure look like pink squiggles? Does healing light look like gold stars?

VIGYANA BHAIRAVA TANTRA METHODS

The latter part of this workbook revolves around one of Tantra's most sacred and beautiful texts, the Vigyana Bhairava Tantra. Starting on page 30 you will find more information about the work and its 112 mental yoga techniques. Throughout the book you will see this symbol followed by a number. This is an invitation to check out a related method in the Vigyana Bhairava Tantra.

Creating A Sacred Practice Space in Your Home

WHY CREATE SACRED SPACE AT HOME?

By dedicating a space in your home or bedroom to meditation, Tantra, or other sacred practices, you are creating a container for the ritual work of self reflection. You will find it easier to drop into these practices if you are able to step away from your daily reality, even if that just means sitting down in front of a little shelf with a candle. The more meaningful sensory cues you can bring in, the more meaningful your dedicated space becomes. Gradually, both your brain and your nervous system start to calm as soon as you get settled in this personal sanctuary.

SPECIAL BELONGINGS

Look around your home for the little tokens of your life that carry deep meaning. It doesn't matter how trivial these items may seem to other people, because this is an expression of your heart, your life, your passion, and your purpose.

If you don't have something obvious, get creative. A paintbrush can represent your love of art, a seashell can connect you to the ocean, a special coin can connect you to abundance, or an animal statuette can remind you of a creature whose qualities you seek to embody.

CALL IN THE ELEMENTS

Cultural references to the elements vary, but they all include Water, Air, Earth, and Fire. Some also include ether or metal. Whichever elements you bring in, understand that it is about honoring the natural world you came from.

Water can be a fountain, or a bowl of water that you change daily as a ritual. Earth can be a plant, or stones. You can even have a plant that lives in water, like a stalk of bamboo. Fire can be candles or incense. Maybe Air will be windchimes, feathers, or simply an open window.

CONSIDER THE SENSES

Tantric philosophy and practice rely heavily on the senses for a reason. They are an access point to the subtle realms and important guides for our energy.

Incorporate scents, gentle lighting, soft fabrics, and even tea and snacks into your sacred space to give yourself the full experience. Let your senses gently guide you from the busy outside world into the quiet safety of your spiritual home.

KEEP IT CLEAN & CLEAR

A powerful sacred space receives attention every day. In much the same way that our bodies become stagnant without use, the energy of our sacred spaces can suffer a similar fate.

This can be as simple as sitting down in your space, burning incense or sage, and rearranging your items until they feel "right". If you are already sitting in your space, you may as well take a few minutes to meditate.

To keep it clean and clear, at least once a year, deconstruct your space and clean everything before building it back up.

Science & Sacred Sensuality

NEUROPLASTICITY

101

Neuroplasticity, the brain's ability to reorganize itself by forming new neural connections, plays a crucial role in accessing sacred sensuality. Through practices like the ones you'll find in this workbook, you can cultivate greater awareness of your body and mind. This heightened awareness allows for the rewiring of neural pathways associated with pleasure, intimacy, and connection. By consciously directing attention towards sensations, emotions, and energy flows, you can break down old patterns of inhibition and shame, fostering a deeper and more authentic experience of sensuality. This process can lead to increased self-acceptance, enhanced emotional regulation, and a more profound connection to both yourself and others.

Building new ways of thinking about pleasure and your body can be challenging at first. Think of it like forming new tracks in a snowy field instead of walking well worn pathways. The first few trips down a new path can feel clunky and awkward, but with each new attempt, the path feels easier and more natural. Have patience, be willing to laugh, and persist through some initial awkwardness.

 To learn more about neuroplasticity check out: "Buddha's Brain: The Neuroscience of Happiness, Love, & Wisdom" by Rick Hanson and Richard Mendius

SYMPATHETIC & PARASYMPATHETIC NERVOUS SYSTEMS

98

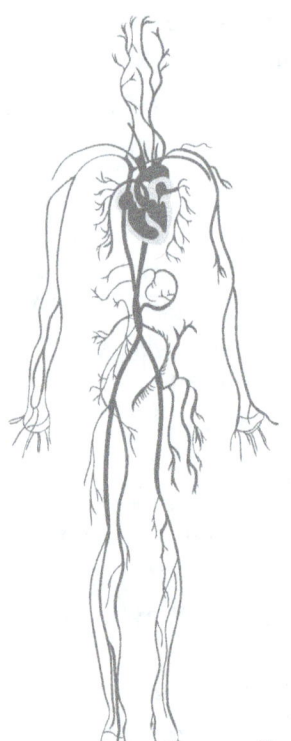

The sympathetic and parasympathetic nervous systems are branches of the autonomic nervous system, responsible for involuntary bodily functions. The sympathetic nervous system, often called the "fight-or-flight" response, prepares the body for action by increasing heart rate, blood pressure, and adrenaline levels. While crucial for survival, excessive sympathetic activation can hinder sexual arousal by creating a state of anxiety and tension.

Conversely, the parasympathetic nervous system, known as the "rest-and-digest" system, promotes relaxation, slows the heart rate, and facilitates digestion. This state is conducive to sexual arousal by allowing for increased blood flow to the genitals and promoting a sense of calm and openness.

In the context of sacred sensuality, cultivating a balanced interplay between these two systems is essential. Practices like the ones in this workbook can help down-regulate the sympathetic nervous system while simultaneously activating the parasympathetic response. This creates an internal environment where pleasure can flourish, allowing for a deeper connection with yourself and your partner.

 For more information about your nervous system check out: "Anchored: How to Befriend Your Nervous System Using Polyvagal Theory" by Deb Dana & Stephen Porges PhD

ELECTROMAGNETISM & THE BODY

28, 93, 99,

Part of exploring sacred sexuality is working with energy, a concept that can feel intangible or woo woo to folks without the right context. The more you can understand and define what it means to "feel the energy" or "work with your body's energy", the more empowered you are the nurture the seed of your own sensuality. Have you ever walked into a room and felt the energy of the space? Have you ever felt like you have a ball of energy in your chest, your belly, or your genitals that wants to burst out of you?

Electromagnetism plays a profound role in the human body, especially in the context of sensuality. Our bodies contain a complex system of electrical signals, from the neural impulses that govern thought and movement to the electromagnetic fields generated by the heart and brain. These bioelectrical energies can be understood as part of a subtle energy field, often explored in sacred sexuality traditions.

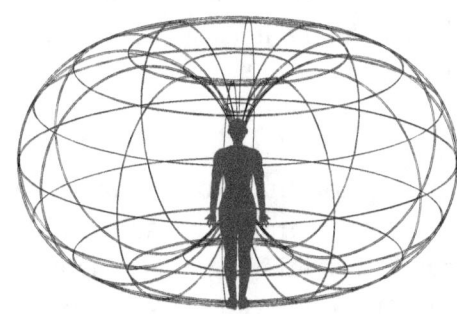

In Tantra, the cultivation and balancing of energy, particularly through practices like the ones in this workbook, are thought to activate the body's energetic currents, enhancing sensory awareness and intimacy. The body's electromagnetic field can also resonate with that of a partner, facilitating a deeper connection, in a process also known as coregulation.

To learn more about electromagnetism and the body check out:
Dr. Robert O Becker - "The Body Electric"
or the group called The Heart Math Institute

CONSCIOUSNESS & QUANTUM WEIRDNESS

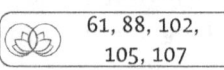
61, 88, 102, 105, 107

In this year 2025, modern scientists still do not know where consciousness comes from or is created. The worldview of Classical Tantra lines up with one modern theory called Panpsychism, or the idea that consciousness itself is an omnipresent layer of reality that is not created, but rather tapped into. In its simplest form, the concept is that all existence is essentially a primordial soup of pure consciousness and pure energy, out of which comes reality as we know it. The locale of your mind is a contraction of that consciousness that individuates into human form, inherently forgetting its nature so that it can purely experience each existence. (That is dense, so maybe just sit with it for while.)

While quantum weirdness is also a lot to unpack in a short space, suffice it to say that quantum science is the study of the smallest particles that make up our reality and it turns out that this tiny world is a pretty strange place! These particles blink in and out of existence, exist as both particles and waves depending on how we look at them, and can even be entangled with one other in ways that defy the speed of light.

Of particular relevance to tantric practice is a phenomenon known as the observer effect. This is the curious effect that researchers have on their subatomic test subjects. Across many experiments, it has been shown that the act of being observed can change the outcome of research on tiny particles. Quantum particles are somehow aware of being watched. Though very inconvenient for scientists, it is a small affirmation to meditators around the world that turning your conscious attention inward on your body can have a dramatic impact. Bringing consciousness to your body's energy is unlocking mysterious forces, so lean into the unknown, suspend your disbelief, and enjoy the ride.

To learn more, check out:
Deepak Chopra, et al. -"Quantum Body: The New Science of Living a Longer, Healthier, More Vital Life"

Vikalpas & Sensuality

The early tantric philosophers recognized something profound: as human beings, we perceive only a narrow slice of reality. We see less than one percent of the light spectrum. Our sense of smell is tens of thousands of times weaker than a dog's. We can't hear what bats hear or feel what trees feel. And most of us can't read each other's minds, so we're left constantly filling in the blanks. Amidst all these short comings, the human mind must write a narrative to make sense of the world.

In tantric philosophy, these mental stories are called Vikalpas. The Western world might call them mental constructs or schemas. Whatever the term, they are the filters that shape our experience and distance us from the raw aliveness of the present moment. In sacred sensuality, vikalpas show up as sexual conditioning, body shame, unresolved emotions, or protective beliefs about what is or isn't safe. They create tension, resistance, and disconnection, both internally and relationally.

The invitation here isn't to suppress the mind or force it into silence. Instead, we gently guide it toward telling more truthful, empowering stories. Stories that are less self-defeating, less limiting, and more alive. You get to choose which version of the truth you live in. And each time you catch a vikalpa in the making and choose to shift it, you create new pathways in the brain. At first it may feel awkward or forced, but with repetition, it becomes a skill.

Meditation, breath work, and other embodied practices don't demand that the mind be quiet, they simply create the space for it to settle. From that stillness, deeper connection becomes possible: to yourself, to your body, to your partner(s), and to something greater than any story could contain.

And here is the deeper tantric insight: every time the mind writes a story, it contracts reality to fit within its lines. Even the most beautiful story is still a narrowing. Core beliefs rooted in fear or lack are especially tight, but all stories, even empowering ones, reduce the mystery of life to something smaller.

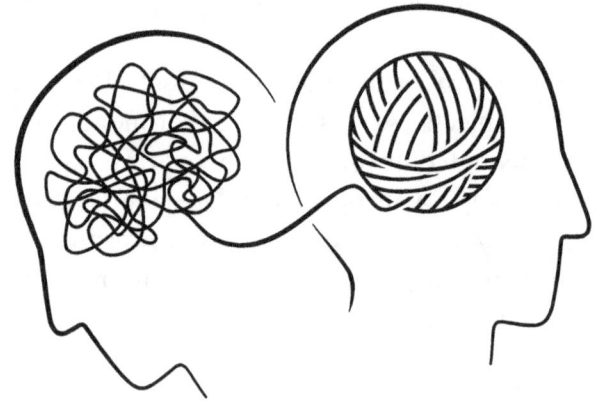

Eventually, the practice becomes less about fixing the story and more about letting it go altogether. Presence doesn't need a script. Reality, at its essence, is truly vast, indescribable, and already complete. All we have to do is turn towards it and bear witness.

And if your inner stories feel especially heavy or painful, working with a therapist or counselor can be a powerful support in unraveling them.

UNSUPPORTIVE VIKALPAS

Some unsupportive mental stories are obvious, while others are more insidious. Here are some signs that your stories are holding you back:

- Negative self talk
- Overly critical thinking
- Getting stuck daydreaming
- Getting stuck reminiscing

- Shame/Fear
- Unrealistic positivity
- Idealizing people or situations
- Arrogance

🖊 Can you think of a Vikalpa that you have around sensuality? (Ex. "I'm a bad lover.")

NIRVIKALPA

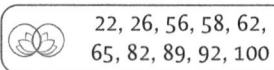

22, 26, 56, 58, 62,
65, 82, 89, 92, 100

Put simply, a Nirvikalpa is thinking that transcends individual consciousness and the material world. A story that is both true and hopeful. Here are signs you are on the right track:

- The story is grounded in something greater than yourself
- It is both accurate and without hopelessness

- It brings you a sense of peace and transcendence
- It is rooted in compassion

🖊 How can you rewrite the above story to be more supportive? (Ex. "I would like to improve my skills as a lover, so I am learning to be the kind of lover I want to be.")

Three Essential Tools for Sacred Sensuality Practice

DEEP BREATH

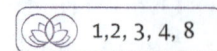 1, 2, 3, 4, 8

Your deep, slow respiration has the power to regulate your nervous system and reset your mind. If you can control the flow of the inhale and exhale then you can activate your nervous system to regain a sense of safety and peace. Breath can also gather up and direct sensation around your body.

TRY THIS:
Breathe as slowly and as deeply as you can without getting lightheaded for 5-10 minutes. Explore your limits.

What do you notice in your body before breathing? And after a few deep breaths?

AWARENESS

25, 53, 55, 64, 78, 83, 87, 92, 107, 112

Where focus goes, energy flows! The effect of loving conscious awareness on the body is well documented. Your body receives your attention like a gift. Gently guide your focus around your body to tune into the myriad of subtle sensations that will guide you through Tantric practice.

TRY THIS:
As you breathe deeply, focus your awareness on your heart. Whatever you find there, meet it with loving kindness.

Which of your senses are you most aware of right now? Which of your senses do you notice least?

VISUALIZATION

7, 36, 61, 74, 79, 80, 94, 97, 102, 106, 109

When your mind is deeply submerged in a visualization, the body believes the imagery to be true and responds accordingly. This is why scary movies make your heart race! This is also why imagination is such a powerful tool for subtle energy work. If you can see it, you can feel it.

TRY THIS:

As you breathe and focus on your heart, imagine a star there, growing with each breath until it expands to surround you.

Call an image to mind that brings you comfort. Don't over think it. It could be anything from a person you love to a cartoon character. As you breath and focus on this visual, what do you notice in your body?

A SENSUAL EXERCISE

48, 50, 51, 54, 95

Find somewhere quiet and comfortable to sit or lay down. Start by closing your eyes and taking several deep, slow breaths. Fill your lungs with as much air as you can while still breathing with ease, and similarly, exhale as much air as you can.

As you continue to breath, move your awareness around your body. Gently notice any areas of tension and take a breath or two to relax those muscles. From there, take notice of any areas of your body that feel good, warm, comfortable, or pleasurable.

Bring your awareness to the pleasurable sensations in your body and imagine that your deep inhale could round up or gather that pleasure. Exhale the positive sensation throughout your whole being, until the visualization expands to fill you completely. Melt into the warmth.

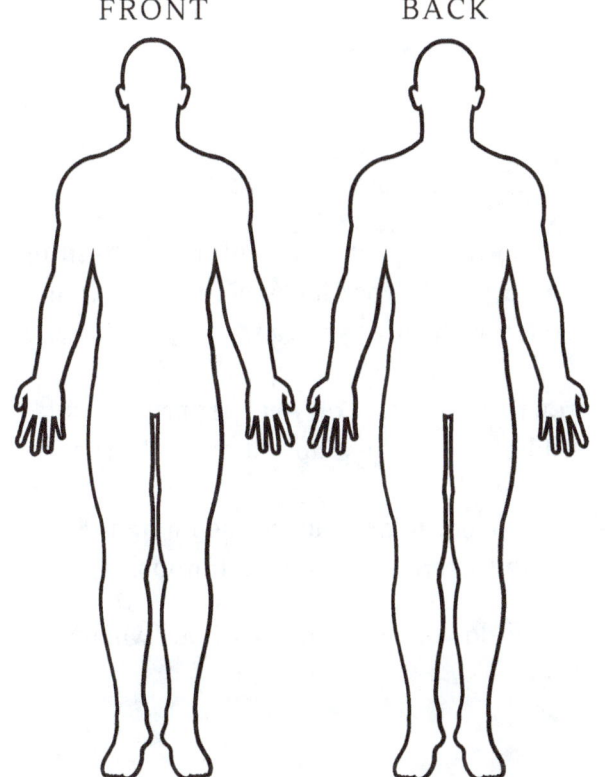

FRONT   BACK

Continue breathing into the sensations you feel and simply observe, as though your mind's eye were a camera documenting what you feel. When you come to a point of completion, open your eyes and gently gaze around you to come present to the outer world once again. Then reflect on what you noticed and complete the exercise by using the diagrams to color, shade, or draw the sensations you felt.   15

Nadis

Nadis, or energy lines, are an essential component of the electromagnetic realm of the body. Much like lightning and magnetic fields, the energy in your body runs along lines. In Vedic science there are 72,000 Nadis that run out of three main channels and there are patterns within that flow of energy. By learning these patterns you can come into greater harmony with yourself and your experience of life.

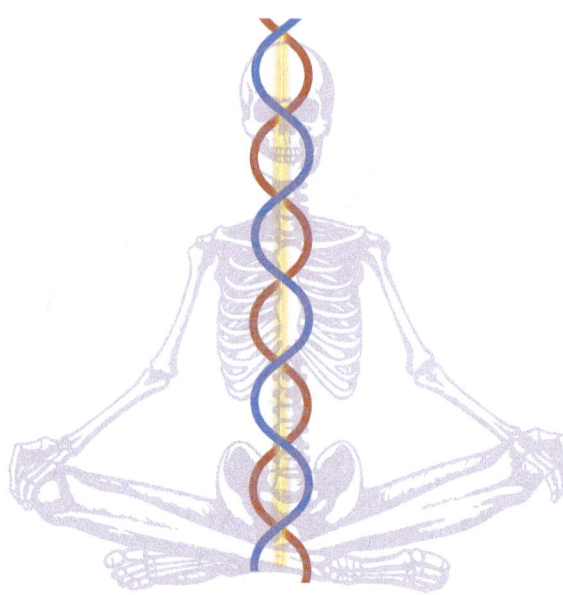

SHUSHUMNA

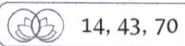 14, 43, 70

This is the central channel that you see in gold on the left. In reality it is transparent because it carries no quality of its own, rather it changes depending on your current state of being and becomes truly activated with spiritual practice.

PINGALA

This channel carries your masculine polarity, which you will learn more about in the following pages. It is your stillness, your consciousness, and your logic, among other qualities. Some people are Pingala dominant.

IDA

This channel carries your feminine polarity, which you will learn more about in the following pages. It is your energy, your intuition, your flow. Some people are Ida dominant.

INNER FLUTE TECHNIQUE

Find somewhere quiet and comfortable to sit upright. Start by closing your eyes and taking several deep, slow breaths. Fill your lungs with as much air as you can while still breathing with ease, and similarly, exhale as much air as you can.

Contract the muscles of your perineum (Mula Bandha). While holding this contraction, inhale through pursed lips like sucking up a straw and visualize energy or air moving up Sushumna.

As you exhale, relax your perineum and visualize the energy moving back down the channel. You can also do this exercise with the intention of uplifting and transmuting sexual energy.

What do you notice in your body when you do this? Do you visualize colors or textures?

Koshas

Another way to understand the energetics of being human is through the Vedic concept of Koshas, or layers of the self. Rather than physical layers, these are concentric layers of your being and your awareness. Think of them as lampshades with your truest self, a spark of ever-glowing conscious energy, at the center. This core light light can permeate all the other layers and empower you through the discomfort they cause. Being overly focused on the outer layers will lead to suffering. As you move through these questions, use a keyword or two to describe your relationship to each one.

66, 83, 84, 89

PHYSICAL BODY (ANNAMAYA)
What do you notice about your physical condition, your abilities or disabilities, your looks, or even your posture?

PRANIC BODY (PRANAMAYA)
What do you notice about your pranic body, or your life force? Are you hungry, tired, sick, in pain? Or are you energized, rested, full, and nourished?

INTELLECTUAL BODY (MANAMAYA)
What do you notice about your mind and emotions? In this worldview, they are two different expressions of the same energy, always in flux. Are they stable? Dynamic? Scary? Safe?

WISDOM BODY (VIJNANAMAYA)
What do you notice about your intuition, your insight, or your meditative space? Do you get stuck here? Do you feel disconnected from it?

BLISS BODY (ANANDAMAYA)
Find the central core witness within you. Do you notice the sense of wonder when you awaken to this layer of your awareness? How does it change your sense of the other layers when you look at them from this perspective?

Chakras

In this lineage, Chakras are energetic vortices that lie at the intersections of Ida and Pingala along the central channel, Sushumna. They are powerful tools for self study and healing. Below you will find some basic information about their qualities as a primer on this complex topic.

CROWN - BLISS FROM WISDOM

Basic Qualities: Shiva, Pure Consciousness, Bliss, Sacred Alignment
Sanskrit: Sahastrara
Color: Purple
Seed Sound: OHM

THIRD EYE - WISDOM FROM TRUTH

Basic Qualities: Intuition, Wisdom, Dreams, Psychic Ability, Sixth Sense
Sanskrit: Ajna
Color: Indigo
Seed Sound: AIEE or AUM

THROAT - TRUTH FROM GRACE

Basic Qualities: Speaking & Hearing Truth, Expression, Communication
Sanskrit: Vishuddha
Color: Blue
Seed Sound: HAM

HEART - GRACE FROM COURAGE

Basic Qualities: Compassion, Forgiveness, Grace, Gentleness, Love
Sanskrit: Anahata
Color: Green
Seed Sound: YAM

SOLAR PLEXUS - COURAGE FROM PASSION

Basic Qualities: Courage, Personal Power, Manifestation
Sanskrit: Manipura
Color: Yellow
Seed Sound: RAM

SACRAL - PASSION FROM PURPOSE

Basic Qualities: Passion, Creativity, Sensuality, Sexuality
Sanskrit: Svadhishthana
Color: Orange
Seed Sound: VAM

ROOT - PURPOSE THROUGH SAFETY

Basic Qualities: Shakti, Pure Energy, Purpose, Belonging, Safety
Sanskrit: Muladhara
Color: Red
Seed Sound: LAM

SEED SOUNDS

5, 37, 42

Using the previous page as a reference, practice acquainting yourself with your Chakras using the seed sounds listed for each one. Try taking a deep inhale and exhaling the seed sound, letting each letter be drawn out for as long as your breath can handle. (ex. Ooooohhhhhhmmmmm) Pause for a deep breath between each seed sound and visualize the sensations you feel in each of these areas. Write down one or two keywords for each Chakra. What do learn about yourself? How does the vibration of each sound feel in your body?

_____

_____

_____

_____

_____

_____

_____

SOLO SENSUAL CHAKRA EXPLORATION

50, 51, 71, 95

Find somewhere quiet and comfortable to sit or lay down. Start by closing your eyes and taking several deep, slow breaths. Fill your lungs with as much air as you can while still breathing with ease, and similarly, exhale as much air as you can.

Place both hands gently on top of your genitals and visualize a warm, grounding energy flowing into your root chakra, located at the base of your perineum. Feel the sensation of pleasure and sensuality rising from the earth, anchoring you to the present moment as you breathe deeply. Linger in your root chakra for 1-3 breaths, infusing this pleasure into your legs and pelvic floor.

When you feel ready, bring your breath, your attention and the visualization of pleasurable sensation up to your sacral chakra. As you inhale, imagine a vibrant, pulsating energy flowing into your sacral chakra, located below your navel. Feel a sense of pleasure and sensuality expanding and deepening within you.

Continue this meditation up through your chakras, lingering at each one for 1-3 breaths. Once you have completed the journey through the chakras, take a few moments to allow the sensations to integrate within you. Feel the energy of pleasure and sensuality flowing freely throughout your body, mind, and spirit. Allow yourself to fully melt into this exercise without a goal or agenda. Use the tools of your breath, your focus, and your sacred imagination to connect deeply with your body from a place of loving exploration and play.

Awakening the Senses

If your body is central to unlocking divine energy, your senses become like your spiritual guides, each one grounding you into a different aspect of reality. They are powerful tools to enhance your ability to be present and spend less time living in your head. Many things, from trauma to a long work day, can detach the mind from the body and make it hard to drop into a sensual space. By working with these guides, you can ease yourself into a softer and more relaxed state of being.

This embodiment can help you love, dance, sing, play, and to just generally live more fully in each moment. A familiar smell can lower your heart rate, a favorite song can pull your mind out of a spiral, and a loving touch can transport you to realms that can't be experienced anywhere else. As you experiment with the following practices, take keen notice. What is your body telling you? What do you learn from these subtle layers of your perception?

If you feel blocked or can't connect with yourself on this level, seek out support in the form of a teacher or counselor. Sometimes we just need an extra set of senses to help us to connect with our own!

SOUND

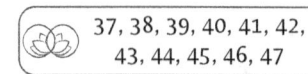
37, 38, 39, 40, 41, 42, 43, 44, 45, 46, 47

What is the loudest thing you hear right now? The quietest?

What sounds do you associate with feeling calm? What sounds do you associate with feeling turned on? What sounds do you associate with feeling playful?

SIGHT

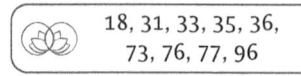
18, 31, 33, 35, 36, 73, 76, 77, 96

What is the most obvious thing you see around you right now? The subtlest?

What sights do you associate with feeling calm? What sights do you associate with feeling turned on? What sights do you associate with feeling playful?

SMELL

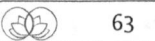

What is the strongest thing you smell right now? The most faint?

What smells do you associate with feeling calm? What smells do you associate with feeling turned on? What smells do you associate with feeling playful?

TOUCH

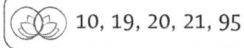

What physical sensation do you notice most right now? And the most subtle?

What touch or texture do you associate with feeling calm? What about feeling turned on? What about feeling playful?

TASTE

What can you taste in your mouth right now? Can you taste anything else?

What tastes do you associate with feeling calm? What tastes do you associate with feeling turned on? What tastes do you associate with feeling playful?

INTEROCEPTION

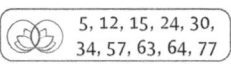

If the other senses tell you about the outside world, interoception is your sense of your inner world.

What is the most obvious thing that you are aware of in your body right now? And the most subtle?

When you get a strong intuition about something, where in your body do you feel it?

Peace Through Polarity

Many spiritual traditions devote teachings to the concept of polarity and paradox because the world can feel so extreme in its opposites that it becomes essential to build an acceptance of times when there are two truths in seeming opposition to one another. Tantra is famous for its embrace of polarity and the concept of non-duality, or transcending black and white thinking.

There is great power in recognizing both ends of a spectrum and embracing everything in between. Very often, when we are miserable or mentally stuck, it is because we have not been embracing the full spectrum of a situation. The following pages and exercises are an opportunity to better understand your own polarity as well as how polarity fits into your journey of sensual fulfillment.

NOT ONLY AM I:	AS ABOVE	I AM ALSO:
MASCULINE		FEMININE
WORKING		PLAYING
DOING		BEING
OUTWARD		INWARD
ANXIOUS		CALM
GIVING		RECEIVING
SCARED		FAITHFUL
ANGRY		KIND
THINKING		FEELING
WOUNDED		HEALING
	SO BELOW	

PELVIC HEART BREATH

Place one hand over your heart and the other over your pelvic bone. Take a deep breath to gather the energy in your heart and exhale it down into your pelvic floor. Inhale the energy back up and down until you can feel a connection forming. As you breathe, practice the mantras above, "Not only am I anxious, I am also calm. Not only do I work, I also play." Include whatever other oppositions come to mind. If this practice is difficult, revisit the page with Three Essential Tools for Tantra Practice.

UNDERSTANDING YOUR OPPOSITES

Contemplate and write down some of the aspects of yourself that are opposites. Reflect on the areas where you can say yes, AND

Not only am I.......   I am also....

_____ anxious _____   _____ calm _____

_____   _____

_____   _____

_____   _____

_____   _____

_____   _____

_____   _____

_____   _____

REFLECTION

17, 59, 65, 69, 74, 89, 111

After practicing the Pelvic Heart Breath and considering your opposing qualities above, what do you notice in your body? What sensations or emotions arise within you as you ponder your own opposing qualities?

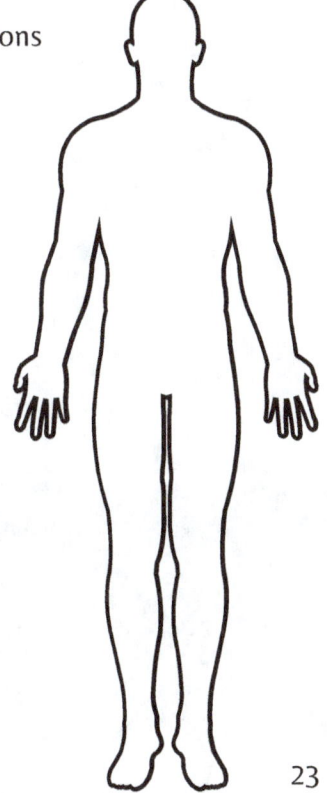

23

Masculine Polarity

In the context of this workbook, and from a tantric perspective, masculine energy is not associated with men or with gender at all. It's a concept used to represent the fundamental energy of consciousness in a state of pure potential, also known as the god, Shiva. Masculine energy is associated with stillness, with transcendence, with the soundless observer, and with the ability to hold space for pure energy, also known as Shakti. Shiva is the light of consciousness in all things.

From a neo-tantric sacred sensuality context, this manifests as an ability to be present, to breathe, and hold space for the big energies that come with sensual energy practices. This is true whether exploring on your own or with a partner. The masculine polarity is the presence you offer to your body in pleasure.

In other sacred sexuality traditions that are often intermingled with Tantra, masculine energy is conversely associated with the positive polarity, outward energy, the active force, the act of giving, and the elements of air and fire. It is important not to get too caught up in these differences because ultimately the whole concept of polarity is somewhat fluid depending on one's culture. If one of these perspectives resonates more with you, then work with it, just be aware of the historical context as well.

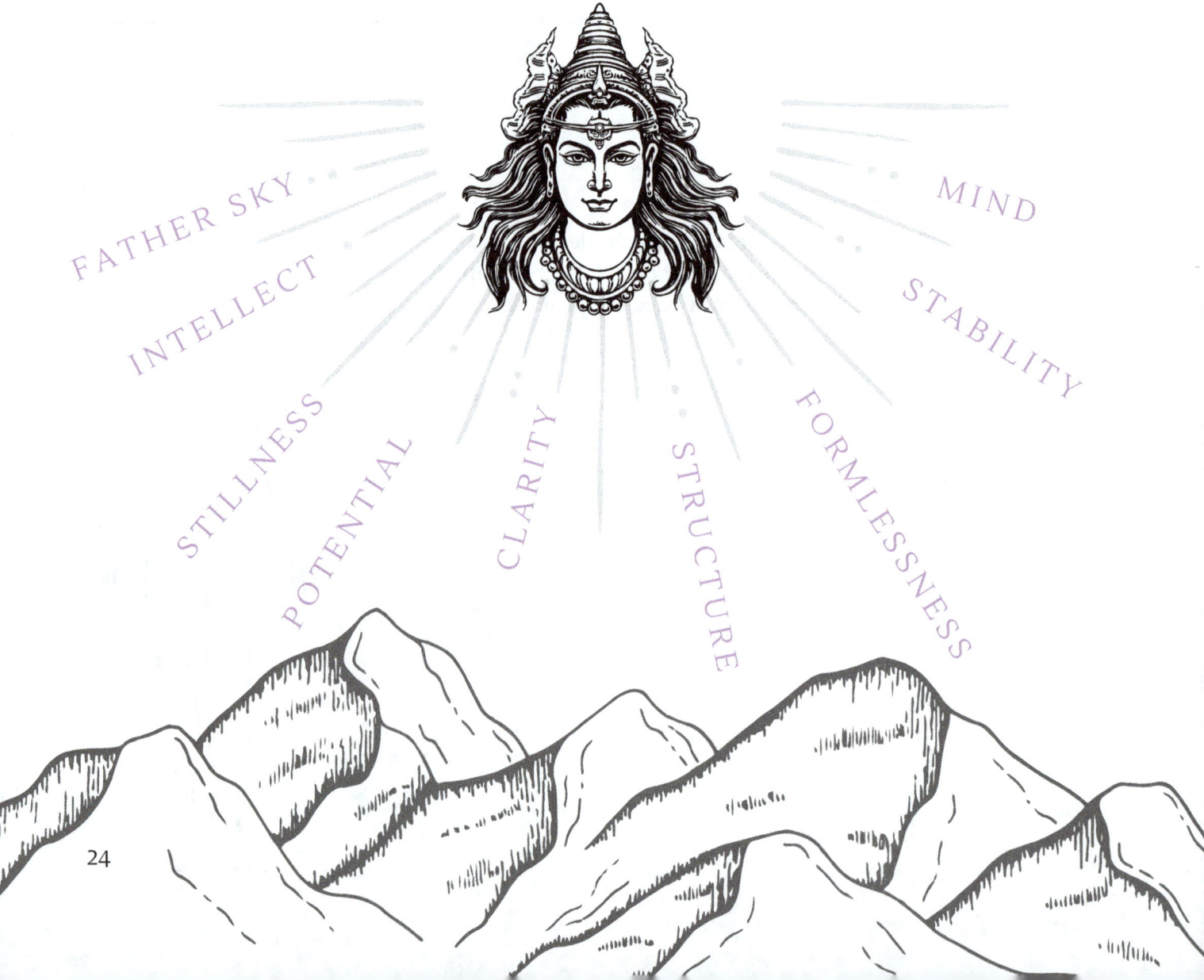

FATHER SKY · INTELLECT · STILLNESS · POTENTIAL · CLARITY · STRUCTURE · FORMLESSNESS · STABILITY · MIND

CLEANSING MASCULINE BREATH

Find somewhere quiet and comfortable to sit upright. Start by closing your eyes and taking several deep, slow breaths. Fill your lungs with as much air as you can while still breathing with ease, and similarly, exhale as much air as you can.

Inhale through the nose and visualize gathering pure conscious awareness from above. If you'd like, visualize Father Sky or Shiva Consciousness with whatever imagery resonates with you.

Exhale through your mouth with a relaxed, open jaw and send energy down and out of your body. Visualize tension, pain, or other stuck energies being released into the Earth. (Ultimately, understand that rather than rejecting these energies, letting go of something means letting go of the resistance to them and allowing them to be a part of your wholeness as a human and as a microcosm of the universe.)

Repeat this breath slowly for a minimum of 5 times for the best effects. Of course, the more time you spend with this exercise the more you will feel its effects.

ACTIVATING MASCULINE BREATH

If you increase the speed of the above exercise, you will find that you can activate the fire of positive polarity in your body and increase your sexual charge. Because breathing quickly can make you lightheaded, I recommend laying on your back with your knees raised. This version can be especially helpful if you find yourself caught in your head during sensual exploration or sex. Allow your visual to carry mental energy down and into the body. Let the mind be immersed in the sensations of this activating breath.

MASCULINE ENERGY REFLECTION

9, 28, 53, 57, 60, 68, 79, 88, 99, 101, 102, 107

 After practicing the above exercises, what do you notice in your body? What feelings, sensations, or emotions come up for you when reflecting on masculine polarity?

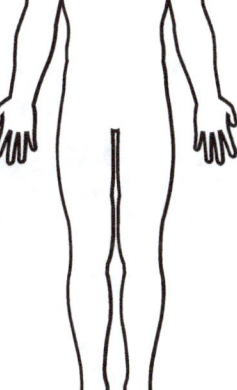

Feminine Polarity

In the context of this workbook, and from a Tantric perspective, feminine energy is not associated with women or with gender at all. It's a term used to represent the fundamental concept of pure energy in a state of expression and movement, also known as the goddess, Shakti. Feminine energy is associated with flow, with embodiment, with manifestation, and with the force of creation. Shakti is the energy that activates Shiva Consciousness from potential to reality. Shakti is the life force that animates all things.

From a neo-tantric sacred sensuality context, this manifests as the purest essence of sexual energy, as Kundalini, a snake of energy spiraled in the root chakra awaiting transformation. Shakti is the pleasure that awakens and moves through your body. When paired with the pure intentions of your Shiva consciousness, this energy can nurture and heal all that it touches. The feminine polarity is the dance of sensuality that rises and falls within you, both alone and when with a partner.

In other sacred sexuality traditions that are often intermingled with Tantra, feminine energy is conversely associated with the negative polarity, inward energy, the passive force, the act of receiving, and the elements of earth and water. It is important not to get too caught up in these differences because ultimately the whole concept of polarity is somewhat fluid depending on one's culture. If one of these perspectives resonates more with you, then work with it, just be aware of the historical context as well.

NURTURING

EMOTION

BODY

MOVEMENT

MOTHER EARTH

MANIFESTATION

DARKNESS

EMOTION

CREATION

SENSUALITY

NURTURING FEMININE BREATH

Find somewhere quiet and comfortable to sit upright. Start by closing your eyes and taking several deep, slow breaths. Fill your lungs with as much air as you can while still breathing with ease, and similarly, exhale as much air as you can.

Inhale through the mouth with a relaxed open jaw, fully receiving pure nourishing energy from the earth below. Visualize bringing supportive energies into your body. Do you need peace? Safety? Play?

Exhale through the nose with a hum. As the hum reverberates through your chest, infuse those nourishing energies into your whole being.

Repeat this breath slowly for a minimum of 5 times for the best effects. Of course, the more time you spend with this exercise the more you will feel its effects.

This breath works beautifully in conjunction with the masculine breath. When you have cleansed your energy with the masculine breath, use this feminine breath to fill the void with more supportive intentions. If you cleansed fear, call in courage. If you cleansed sorrow, call in joy.

ACTIVATING FEMININE BREATH

You can work with this breath to increase your connection with the energy and pleasure in your body, while inviting relaxation in your pelvic floor that allows energy to move more freely around your body.

Lay on your back with your knees bent and practice the breath above.
On an inhale, lift your hips up and on an exhale drop them back down.
As you breathe, feel your hips loosen and allow your body to move like a snake.

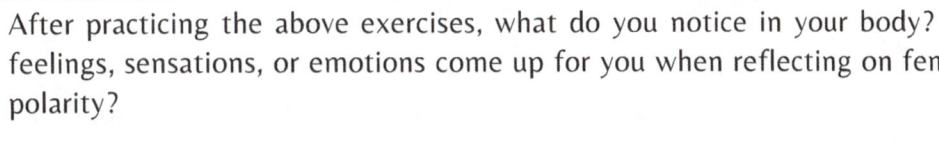
20, 24, 49, 50, 63, 64, 67, 76, 81, 87, 98, 110

FEMININE ENERGY REFLECTION

After practicing the above exercises, what do you notice in your body? What feelings, sensations, or emotions come up for you when reflecting on feminine polarity?

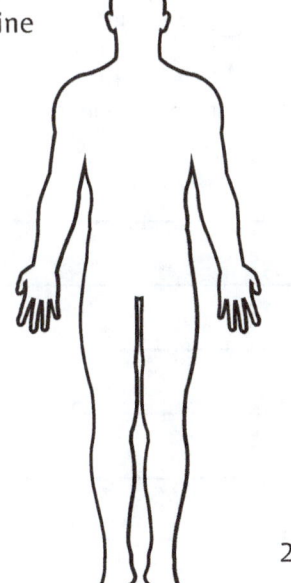

Polarity in Partnership

While much of this workbook is dedicated to personal practice, each one of these concepts can dovetail into the dynamics of a partner practice for a whole new level of experiencing. Try any of the previously mentioned practices with your partner while sitting across from one another and sharing the experience. It can be easy to lose focus on the relevance of polarity by understanding it as a binary when in reality it encompasses both ends of the spectrum, both you and me, and everything in between.

When practicing intimacy with a partner, much less living together and navigating daily life, learning the nuance of polarity can be truly transformative. The space in between lovers is where all the magic happens. The practices below can help you two to dissolve into a moment together and find a space of warmth and peace.

EYE GAZING

13, 18, 29, 32, 48, 56

Sit or stand comfortably across from your partner. Start by holding hands, closing your eyes, and taking three deep breaths together in unison. On the fourth breath, open your eyes and gently gaze into the eyes of your partner. Meet one another with love and safety. If you see pain or fear, meet it with love. If you see love, meet it with more love. Continue eye gazing for at least two minutes or ten breaths.

Eye gazing can bring up some really intense feelings! It can be hard to hold all that energy, so be conscious of breathing together in unison and let long exhales move the energy that feels too big to hold. Try the Cleansing Masculine Breath here. When you're more comfortable, try this exercise with the Feminine Nurturing Breath. If you get the giggles, sometimes this is actually from the anxiety of being seen. Let yourself have them for a moment and then return to long deep breaths and ground into love, safety, and sensation.

EYE GAZING REFLECTION

When eye gazing, what sensations or emotions come up for you two? Each partner list 5 keywords below, and then try eye gazing again to see if you notice a difference after pausing to reflect.

_____   _____

_____   _____

_____   _____

_____   _____

_____   _____

CIRCULAR BREATH

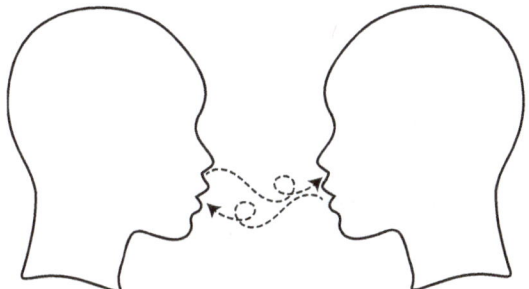

This breath is an energy exchange that embodies the process of transcending duality, of uniting opposites, of dancing in the "in-between".

It is about finding a breathing rhythm together, which can be a tricky practice to learn without a guide, so be patient with yourselves and seek help if it feels like a struggle.

• Sit closely and comfortably across from one another.
• You can eye gaze or you can also close your eyes and rest your foreheads together.
• One of you start by taking a deep inhale and exhaling as though giving your breath to your partner.
• As the first partner exhales, the second partner inhales, receiving the energy.
• Now do the same in reverse.
• Inhale one another's exhale in a natural, slow flow of breath.
• Find a rhythm with both partners breathing comfortably and in sync- one's inhale to the other's exhale. Linger in this sweetly energetic space and melt into presence together.

CIRCULAR BREATH REFLECTION

When trying out this breath, what sensations or emotions come up for you two? Each partner list 5 keywords below, and then try it again to see if you notice a difference after pausing to reflect.

_____   _____

_____   _____

_____   _____

_____   _____

_____   _____

YAB YUM

To deepen the beautiful practice of circular breathing, try sitting in the yab yum position. This famous image represents the union of divine Shiva masculine and divine Shakti feminine, or the union of pure consciousness and pure energy, as you will likely feel when you try it.

Some things to consider:
• Whoever is in the feminine position, atop the other partner's lap, may want to sit on a pillow for comfort.
• Neither partner needs to have their legs crossed if this is uncomfortable.
• Try to keep your spines straight.
• If you can do so while maintaining the flow of breath, try placing a hand on your partner's heart, or even using the hands to gently stroke one another.

TIPS FOR TANTRIC TOUCH

The giving and receiving of touch can be a surprisingly difficult aspect of romantic relationships for a multitude of reasons. Sometimes you may feel self conscious about "doing it the right way" or you may have grown up in a home without a lot of affection so touch feels foreign to you. You may even have a partner with a history of trauma who is only comfortable with certain kinds of physical contact.

Many of the tantric touch methods that you'll come across are from Neo-Tantra more than Classical Tantra. It is rooted in a deep presence to both the giver and the receiver, and it encourages an attitude of exploration, curiosity, and sacred play.

PLAY

One of the biggest killers of sensuality is the pressure to perform. Often this pressure comes from within, born out of a desire to fulfill your image of an ideal lover. So the suggestion here is to remove any goals, even pleasure and especially orgasm. Give yourself and your partner permission to be playful. This means being vulnerable, letting go of outcomes, and accepting both of you exactly as you are.

TIP: Place your hand over your partner's hand and guide it around your body in places that you like to be touched. Press on their hand to indicate more pressure, lighten it to indicate less.

EXPLORE

With sensual touch, there can be a tendency to focus on the genitals and breasts, but from a tantric perspective, the whole body is an erogenous zone. Imagine you are seeing your partner's body for the first time and explore it deeply. Give appreciation to the parts of the body that are usually ignored. Massage a pinky toe, stroke the back of the knee, or trace the lines of the ribs.

TIP: Try body mapping together. Use green, yellow, and red to color in areas of your body that you like or don't like to be touched. Let this be a guide for your exploration.

BREATHE

As mentioned above, tantric touch is rooted in deep presence to your beloved. The best way to stay deeply present and out of your Vikalpas is to stay connected to your breath. Let your breath guide your experience.

TIP: If giving, breathe into each movement as though you can pass love through your hands with long, whole body strokes. If receiving, breathe deeply into each sensation. Make noise on long exhales to give your partner feedback.

THE FIVE MAGIC HOURS

Tantra is a practice of turning off autopilot and becoming more conscious in each given moment. The following guide, created by marriage and sexuality researcher, John Gottman, invites you as a couple to put aside any differences for just a moment and be gentle with one another. Both people need to feel seen, heard, and supported in love. It is natural for life to pull two people apart and with small moments like these you can reconnect into the foundation of presence and love that brought you together in the first place.

1. PARTINGS 10 minutes each work day (50 minutes total)

Before leaving for work or starting your weekdays, take ten minutes to be present to one another and find out what your partner is planning on doing that day.

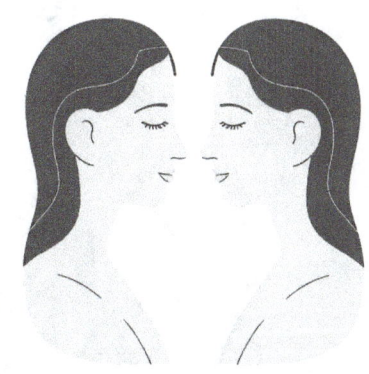

2. REUNIONS 20 minutes each workday (1 hour 40 minutes total)

When you two reconnect at the end of your workdays, take twenty minutes to greet each other lovingly and hear about what happened during the day. Take the time to put down devices and really tune in.

3. APPRECIATION 5 minutes everyday (35 minutes total)

Take a few minutes everyday to tell your partner something that you admire or appreciate about them. It can be something large or something mundane, just be sure to express gratitude and love.

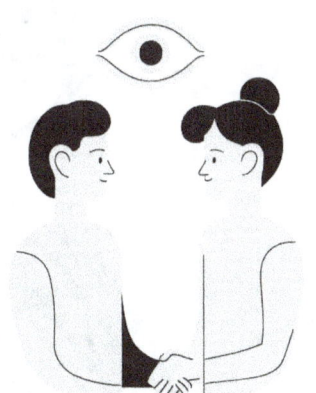

4. AFFECTION 5 minutes everyday (35 minutes total)

Take a few minutes everyday to share some physical affection with your partner. This could be kissing, cuddling, hugging, or even just holding hands and breathing with your heads together.

5. DATE 2 hours every week

Find the time once a week to spend two uninterrupted hours together. This is a great time to practice the exercises you find in this workbook or just take a long walk and have a meal together.

FEELING TOO DISCONNECTED TO TRY THIS?

If you find yourselves struggling to connect during these five hours, that's okay! Consider reaching out a couples therapist, counselor, or coach for support.

EBusse
www.erikabusse.com
IG: @ebusse.art

Vigyana Bhairava Tantra

 The text that inspired this section is called the Vigyana Bhairava Tantra, a Kashmir Shaiva writing from the 7th century that is central to the tantric worldview and ideology.

A portion of the work contains a conversation between Shakti, the divine feminine representing pure energy, and Shiva, the divine masculine representing pure consciousness. In a beautiful garden, Shakti asks Shiva, "Oh Shiva! What is the nature of our reality?" He answers her with 112 meditations that can reveal the sacred beauty underlying our daily reality.

These meditations are from just one sacred text in a long lineage. Their function was to show the practitioner that, all other practices aside, it is possible to awaken to the true nature of reality using only the mind itself. Often referred to as inner yoga, or dharanas, the techniques included here teach understanding how powerful each being is. They explore key concepts of breath, awareness, visualization, duality, polarity, subtle energy, presence, awe, spaciousness, perception, and stillness. They seek to teach you how it feels be both deeply focused and deeply relaxed in order to create the ideal conditions for awakening to your blissful center that is always safe and always okay.

Here I am, offering this project as a light skinned, biracial, multi-faith woman in America. Who am I to interpret such a sacred ancient text? The answer is that I am just one person, of millions, whose life has been changed by the reflections contained in the Vigyana Bhairava Tantra. My introduction to this work was in my first month of learning Tantra with Denise. She instructed me to buy Osho's Book of Secrets and to use it to deepen my understanding of the work we were doing together. Since then I have spent fifteen years of research and practice with these teachings, both personally and professionally. They have helped me soothe many wounds and glean wisdom from the deepest sorrows.

So with that background, I share the following pages with a deep humility. I used Paul Reps and Osho's numbering of the meditations for simplicity's sake and I tried to connect the concept of each technique to familiar words and images that would ignite a spark in the reader, while opting to leave some of the more esoteric teachings as a bit of a mystery to be digested through meditation. My professional practice is called Subtle Seed, in part because I believe the smallest seed you plant in your heart has the potential to infinitely change your life. Each one of the following meditations is its own seed, carrying an idea that when fully realized, can bring real peace and understanding to the practitioner.

I give this as a work of love that fluttered down and bubbled out over many years. It is my greatest hope that this section can help even just one person find healing, ignite an esoteric journey, or connect with a more meaningful existence. Below are a few wonderful resources on the Vigyana Bhairava Tantra for those who want to explore this text in a deeper way:

- Swami Satyasangananda Sarawati -"Sri Vijnana Bhairava Tantra- The Ascent"
- Dr. Mark Dyczkowski - www.anuttaratrikakula.org/vijnana-bhairava/
- Paul Reps - "Zen Flesh Zen Bones"
- Lorin Roche - "The Radiance Sutras"
- Osho -"The Book of Secrets"
- Christopher D. Wallis- www.tantrailluminated.org

1. Observe the pause as your chest rises, but before it falls.
And again as your chest falls, but before it rises.

To bring your attention to the gap in between your breaths is to press a pause button on your life. In that gap the vital air exchange between you and the world ceases completely. What do you notice in the pause? What does your heart do? Your mind? Your lungs?

Meditation techniques often bring your attention to the inhale and the exhale- the inward and outward flow of life force. This practice is an invitation to focus on something different, something more subtle. In the pause when your diaphragm shifts its motion, there is a moment that becomes a timeless portal into the microcosm of the human experience.

This momentary gap can be a quiet refuge for your mind, as often as a thousand times a day. An opportunity for your inner world to rest and catch up to your outer experience. A chance to step out of mental storytelling and just be present, even if only for a moment.

WHAT DO YOU NOTICE?

FRONT   BACK

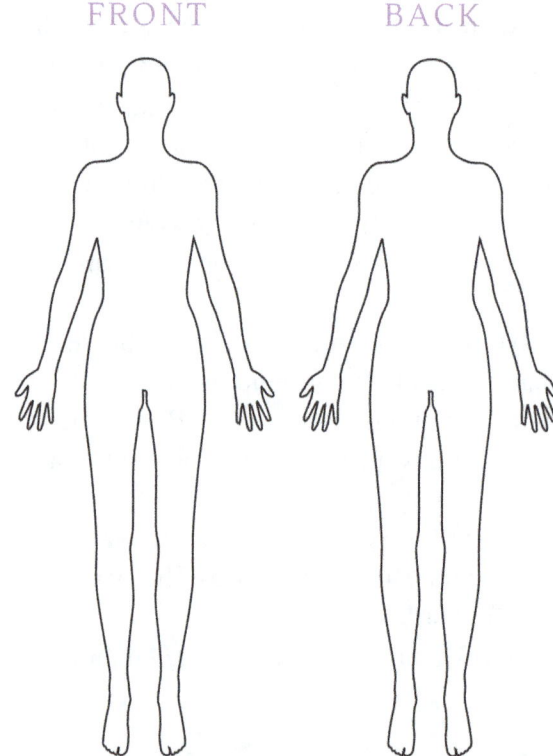

34

2.
Notice an inhale turning into an exhale
and again as it turns back.
Let the turning show you.

Visualize what happens when air moves in and around the body. Have you ever seen images of the human lungs? Can you visualize this essential organ that processes the life-sustaining gift of air? How does the air move? How do your muscles move as an inhale turns into an exhale? Dive deep into that turning motion to understand a spiritual truth.

Envision the shifting nature of air as it reaches the farthest depths of your lungs and then turns back around to return to the external world. Follow one oxygen molecule all the way into your bloodstream. See the whole journey as the air twists and turns its way around your body before exiting.

See the ways that you yourself turn like the breath within you. See how many things in the world turn this way- the waves, the clouds, the seasons, the leaves, the migrating birds. See the whole world turning back and forth. Feel this sacred dance with each breath you take.

WHAT DO YOU NOTICE?

FRONT   BACK

3. When the inhale and the exhale meet, you too fuse into the moment.

Take a few deep, slow breaths and be careful to notice the moment when your inhale and exhale embrace before parting ways. The air itself does not distinguish between in and out, it just merges and continues on its path. The distinction between inhale and exhale is simply another human illusion.

The whole tantric philosophy of duality is contained in this one simple technique. Transcend duality through unity. You don't have to be limited to one or the other, calm or anxious, masculine or feminine, doing or being, giving or receiving. In truth you are all the things, whether you like to admit to it or not. So in the embrace between inhaling and exhaling, feel a moment of wholeness.

Like breath you can also flow smoothly into and out of divine reality. You can experience this in the moment when your inhale and exhale meet, fusing into one another. In that space, your consciousness and energy can expand beyond the illusion of separation. As they fuse, you too fuse in that ephemeral moment of bliss, of divine seeing.

WHAT DO YOU NOTICE?

FRONT   BACK

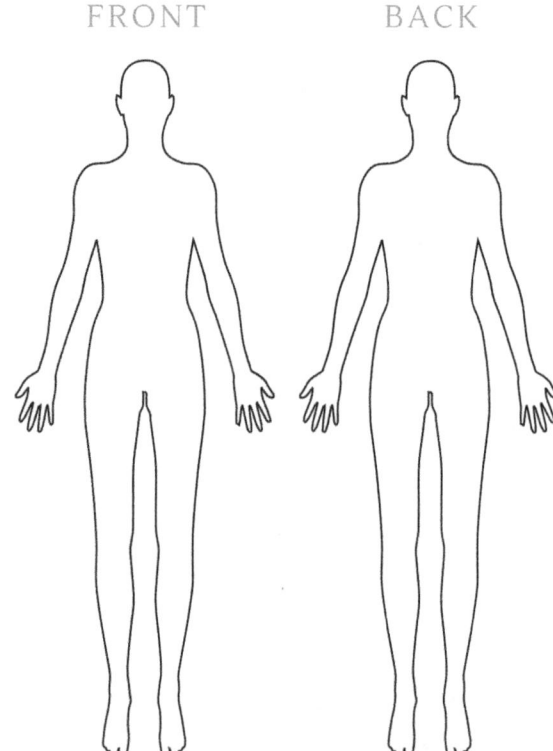

4. Whenever your breathing stops,
give awareness to the pause.
Find the peace in the stillness.

Breath often stops at peak emotional moments, both joyous and strained. Becoming aware of this can help you to reconnect, not only to the movement of breath, but to your emotional center.

Modern science has repeatedly reaffirmed the ancient knowledge that the breath is deeply connected to the nervous system and can help to regulate your emotions back into a calm state. As the breath slows down, particularly the exhale, so too does the heart. And as it slows the entire body is soothed into into safety.

If you are agitated and your breathing stops, take a moment to embrace the pause and reset into a slower inhale and exhale. Use the stop to mentally reflect on the present moment and return to your conscious center.

If you happen to be in such a calm, pleasurable place that the breathing stops, linger in the pause to deeply explore the limitations of your lungs. Linger in the pause and melt into peaceful quietude.

WHAT DO YOU NOTICE?

FRONT   BACK

5. Bring attention to your third eye and let the sensation expand to fill you completely.

With a deep breath, bring your focus to the middle of your forehead just above the eyebrows. This place is the seat of the soul, the origin of dreams, the center of intuition. It is the place in your body where you can connect with the world beyond what you can see and physically sense.

This basic exercise is about guiding awareness, energy, and breath around your body. It can serve even the most advanced practitioners to reconnect to their centered intuition.

First, notice the sensation when you bring your awareness to the third eye. What does it feel like? Does it tingle or glow with a lightness? When you connect to this sensation, feel it move throughout your whole being. Let your whole self tingle, become light, and connect to your divine intuition. Allow your body to feel the true expansive nature of reality. Should this powerful practice overwhelm you, go outside and breathe with your bare feet on the earth.

WHAT DO YOU NOTICE?

FRONT   BACK

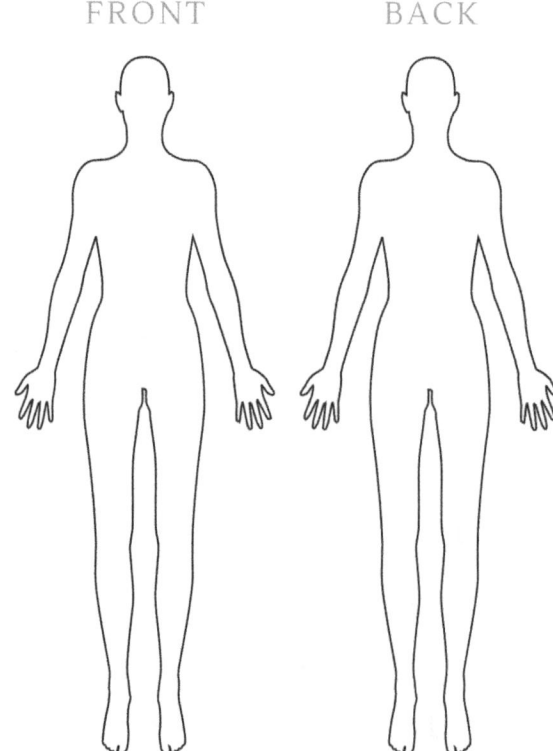

6. Become conscious after stopping one task and before starting another.
Let the pause renew you.

In constantly jumping from one activity to another, you can easily lose sight of the present moment. Some meditations ask the practitioner to stop and be in stillness for an extended period of time. However, this technique just asks you to pause and breathe for a moment in the time between all the things you do in a day.

It asks you to interrupt the story of your day to bring your awareness to your body, mind, and spirit. If you need, take this moment to self soothe and come back to center. If you feel at peace, take this moment to let the goodness permeate you completely.

Take advantage of this technique a dozen times a day. Let it become a way of life to pause for a breath and awaken after doing the dishes, after a drive, or after a phone call. Let these pauses between tasks be a way to continuously fill yourself with the warm, ever-glowing light of consciousness.

WHAT DO YOU NOTICE?

FRONT   BACK

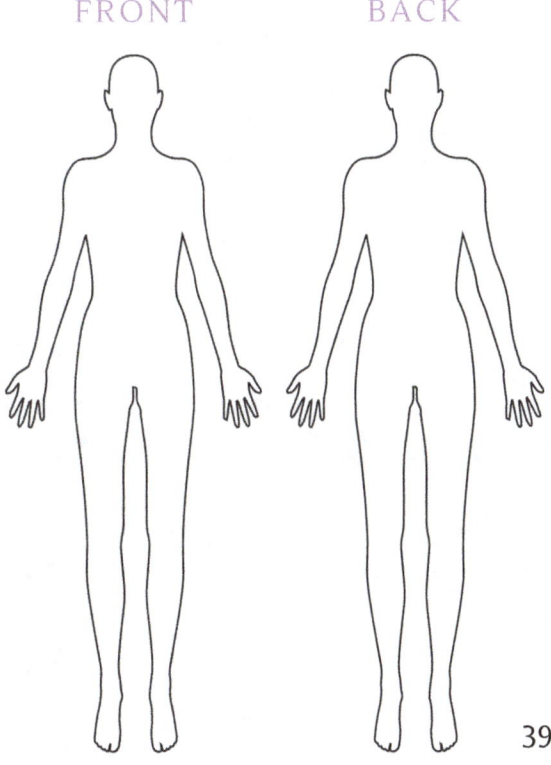

7. Breathe attention from your forehead
into your heart as you drift asleep,
thus awakening in your dreams and more.

This technique is aimed at capturing the effervescent intuitive powers of the third eye so that they gently rain down into the heart as your consciousness drifts from a waking state to sleeping. It teaches you to ground mental energy into the body, redirecting consciousness into the center of feeling, which allows for a more full and honest experience of reality.

It is suggested that practicing this technique regularly will allow the practitioner to awaken in dreams. By becoming lucid in this deep state of mind, you become more capable of tapping into your own latent psychic and intuitive abilities.

In this technique, remember Tantra teaches that the inner world is a microcosm of the whole universe. As you explore your own consciousness you awaken to powerful truths about the vast cosmos underlying your daily life. By inviting this rich energy into the heart, you invite divine light to fill your sleep with its gentle wisdom.

WHAT DO YOU NOTICE?

FRONT   BACK

8. Appreciate the swirling of each breath, as though watching whirlpools in a stream.

Envision your breath moving as though it were water flowing through you like a stream. As you exhale see the warm air leaving your body and swirling into the ambient air around you. Feel the breath hit your hand and see it swirl as it bounces off your skin. Visualize the splash of a quick breath and the flood of a deep sigh.

As though you could drink it, fully take in a gulp of air and feel it spill into your lungs, refreshing you like a long, cool drink of life force energy. Understand the nature of that energy is creative, expansive, and healing. With each breath you can be awash in pure potential.

In the same way that it is soothing to sit by a creek and watch the currents, so too can you find peace from sitting with the ever-swirling motions of your breath. You can envision simple physics. The air that gives you life is constantly exchanging between your inner and outer worlds, moving like a liquid, permeating the whole body.

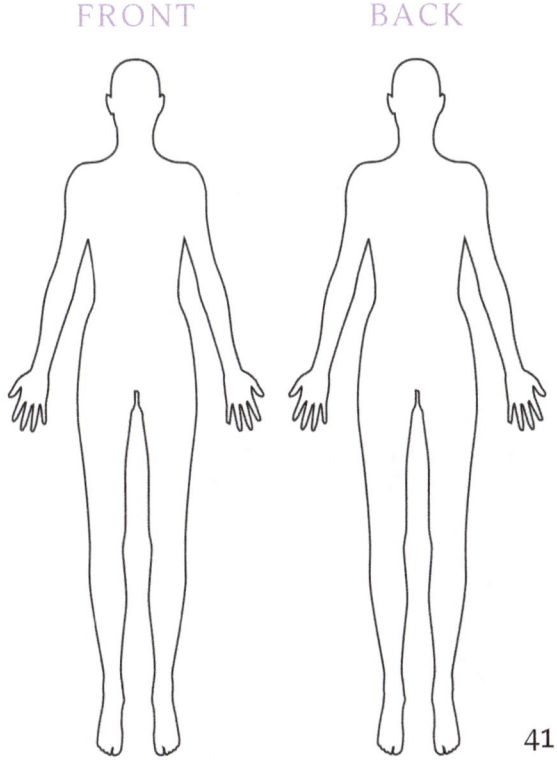

WHAT DO YOU NOTICE?

FRONT   BACK

9. Be still as though you are dead. Stare without moving. Reflect.

This is such a simple concept of a meditation at its core. It calls you to daydream the present moment, to listen to your body as it reacts to physical stillness. Ask yourself to linger in repose. Do you melt into its quiet waters? Does stillness stir up a fearful or twitchy energy in you?

Many people today are struggling with this concept in a world that encourages constant movement. Even moments of rest are filled with screens that keep the mind perpetually engaged in, even addicted to stimulation.

This practice is a conscious decision to just stop. Whether laying, sitting, or even standing- just stop. Be still. Stare off into space and let the world move on without you. If an ant crawls on your foot, let it. If your mind wanders, gently inhale it back into this moment of tranquility. Let the eyes fall flat and passively stare. In the pause, reflect on the miracle of existence, on what it means to simply be.

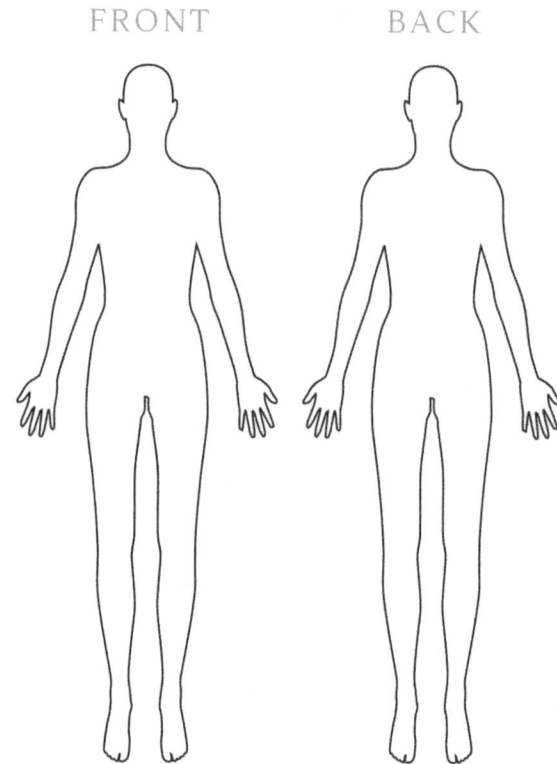

WHAT DO YOU NOTICE?

FRONT   BACK

42

10. Let gentle touch overtake your awareness. Feel the whole universe in your nerves.

Giving and receiving touch has the power to pull you fully into the present moment. It can be a gentle guide to bring your mind into alignment with your breath and your body.

You store so much of your conscious experience in your physical body. Your life story, good and bad, lives in your muscles and in your very DNA. To receive touch is to truly be seen in this story and to give touch is to truly see another in theirs. A still hand connecting with another body says, "I see you. I witness you. I love you." Moving hands can say, "Let me help you transform this story that you hold within. Let me help you tell your truth."

Tantra teaches that each soul, each human body, is a microcosm of the universe and through physical connection you are able to witness that vast reality, including all its wisdom. Not only do you get to witness the realms of subtle energy, but your touch also speaks the language of this mysterious aspect of reality.

WHAT DO YOU NOTICE?

FRONT   BACK

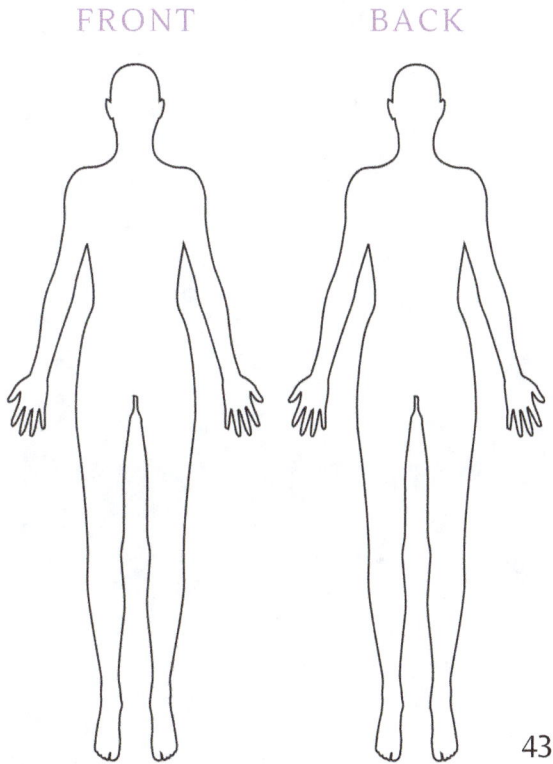

43

11. Disconnect from your senses as if turning to stone.

Intentionally separate your awareness from your sensory reality. Let all things become distant from your consciousness. Numbed touch, muted sound, blinded vision, dulled taste. What is the experience at your center when there is no outside input?

If your senses are your access to the world, and its access to you, what happens when you turn them off? One by one, turn them off. First imagine not hearing whatever you are hearing right now. Then imagine suddenly not smelling what you smell. Then your vision drops off. Then not even the taste in your mouth or the clothing on your skin remain. Not even the sensation in your muscles and your organs within you.

Who are you without your senses? What does your experience become and how are you experiencing it? Perhaps you do become a stone, simply passive and perception-less. A pebble, gently tossed down a riverbed, ever shaped by the water that you cannot see, hear, taste, smell, or touch.

WHAT DO YOU NOTICE?

FRONT   BACK

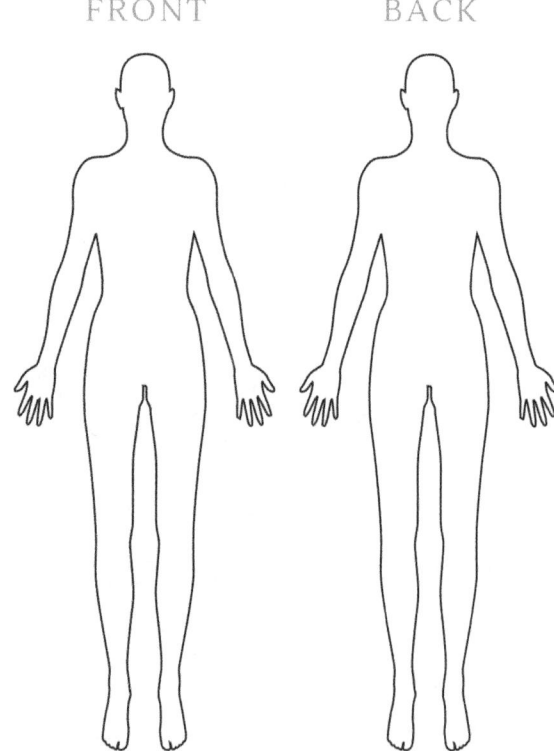

44

12. Levitate in mind and feel it in body. Let go of all weight.

What does weightlessness feel like? Imagine. Take a guess. Feel it on all levels, your mind, your muscles, your bones, and even your organs.

This is a powerful technique to hone your skill of visualization. Remember, if you clearly imagine something, either positive or negative, the mirror neurons in your brain send messages to your body as though it were really happening. This is an underused super power contained in every human.

Convince your mind and every cell in your body that you are growing ever lighter with each breath. Each exhale sheds a little more weight until you can feel your body floating above the surface you're on, above the surface of the earth.

All the weight you carry in life, lifted off you with each breath. You may even feel an ebb and flow to this floating as your mind wants to wander, but gently bring it back to linger in the lightness. Float with your breath as long as you can.

WHAT DO YOU NOTICE?

FRONT   BACK

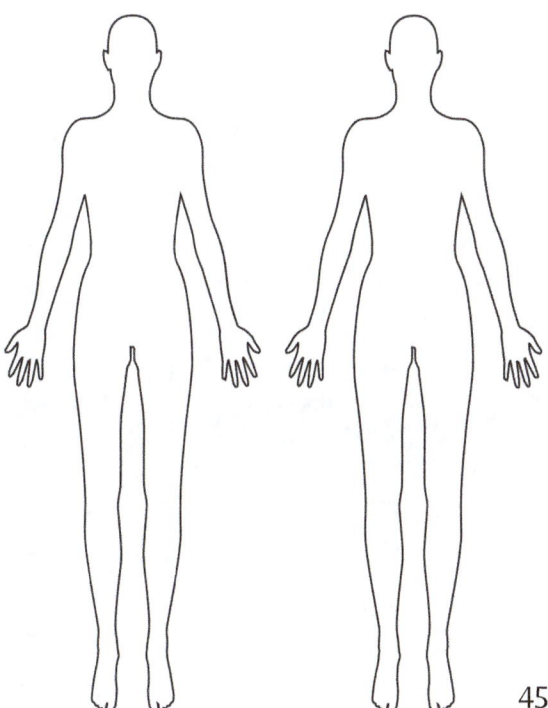

13. Give your attention fully to one point or object until its center merges with yours.

Focus your awareness on a singular object or point in space and wrap your consciousness around it. Fully perceive this point or object, not just in passing. Imagine the very nature, or is-ness, of a shirt, of a stain on the wall, of a plant, or of a crystal. What qualities does it hold? What would it be like to experience the world as that object?

As everything in existence, aside from you and this object, fades into the background, feel yourself connecting to it on a quantum level. Connect to the object so fully that even the edges of your being begin to blur, even the edges of the object blur.

Breathe into this meditation. Draw it out until there are no edges and the only distinction that you see is the unique essence or vibration of both you and the object, waving and blending. Draw it out until these vibrations overlap and merge, until all vibrations, all waves, all frequencies merge into one soundless sound, one waving ocean of conscious existence.

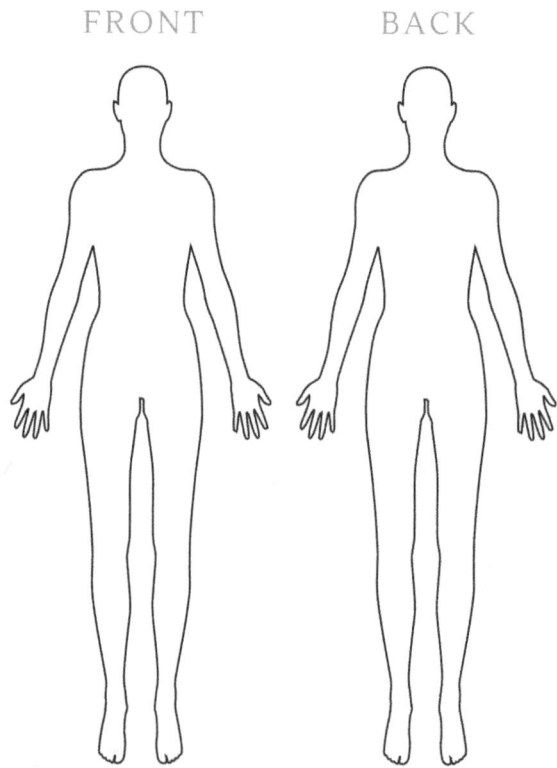

WHAT DO YOU NOTICE?

FRONT   BACK

14. Lengthen and straighten your spinal cord. Through this tether body and spirit align.

Sit or stand as straight as you can, feel the stretch as though your crown could touch the sky. Clear and open the path for spiritual energy to move through your spine and transform you.

This central channel, Sushumna, is a unifying and blending pathway. Envision duality, masculine and feminine, light and dark, and many others wrapping around this cord in a double helix. One side of that helix moves upward while the other moves down. In the center lies Sushumna. Let the visual of this exercise align the grand duality of body and spirit.

By connecting to this cord within, you can can access powerful energetic support through deep breathing and visualizing feelings and thoughts that don't support you moving down into the earth to be fertilizer for the nourishing energy that then rises back up to feed your personal growth. From this tether you can become your own healer, your body can be your teacher, and you can access divine peace.

WHAT DO YOU NOTICE?

FRONT   BACK

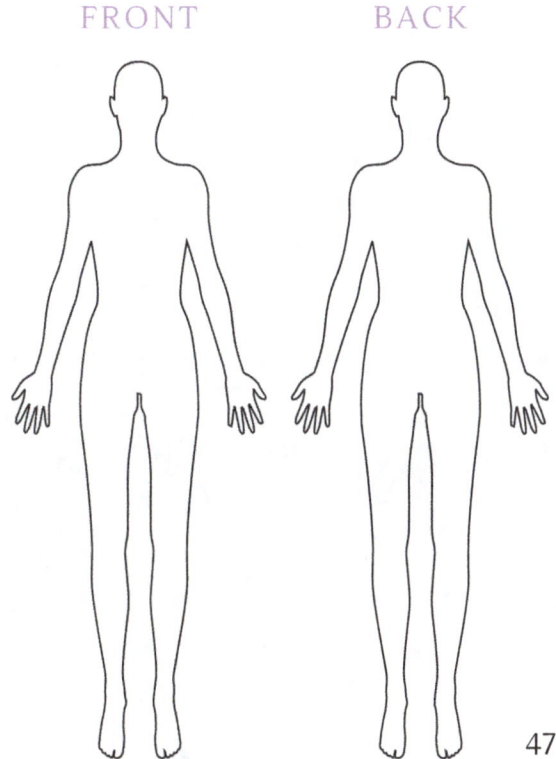

15.

Close the eyes, ears, nose, and mouth.
Notice as the third eye awakens.

Enter into childlike exploration of the human experience by closing all the openings on your head. What do you experience when you do this? Can you hear and feel your muscles vibrate? Can you feel the vital pranic breath energy trying to both enter and escape?

With no other avenue to flow, this essential primordial energy collects in your third eye. As you draw out this experience, what information do you receive in your third eye? Is it visual? Audio? Sensory? What aspect of the subtle world do you connect with here?

Notice the sensations that develop in the rest of your body as your intuitive center arises from its slumber. Akin to plunging yourself under water, a part of you or perhaps all of you, enters into a space of stillness. A deep pause in which your only choice is to turn your gaze inward to witness the chasm of your inner world. Turn on interoception and linger for a while in your personal microcosm.

WHAT DO YOU NOTICE?

FRONT   BACK

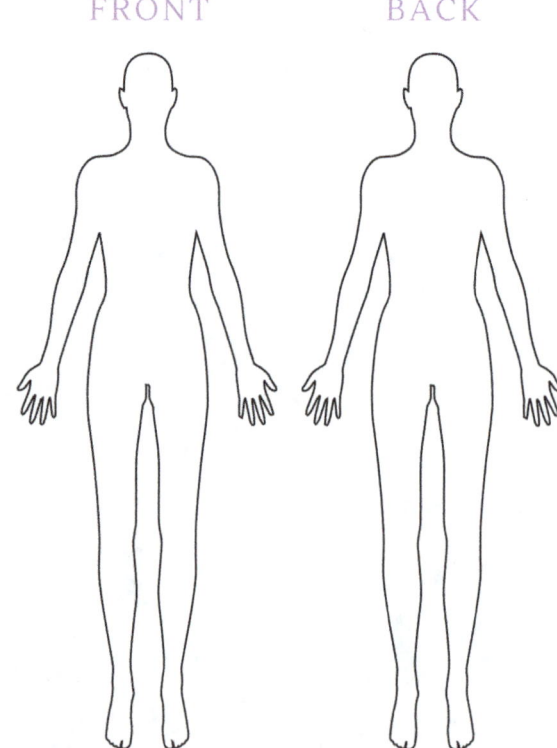

The mind has a way of accidentally destroying the essence of what it is processing. Your senses get masticated by the translation system of the brain. What does it mean to purely experience a sense from the heart, with no story around it, no translation?

Imagine as though you were an animal without language or social constructs, without all the stories that your human brain writes to make sense of reality. Consider instead if the sound of singing birds could permeate directly into the vessel of your heart. If the taste of your favorite food melted from your tongue straight to your heart, filling it with satisfaction.

Bypassing the mental understanding of the senses allows you to unplug from the mental stories that prevent you from fully experiencing the world. How different is your experience of smell, sound, taste, and touch when you let go of all the beliefs they trigger? Do you get a fresh perspective? Which of these stories actually serves you? Find clarity here.

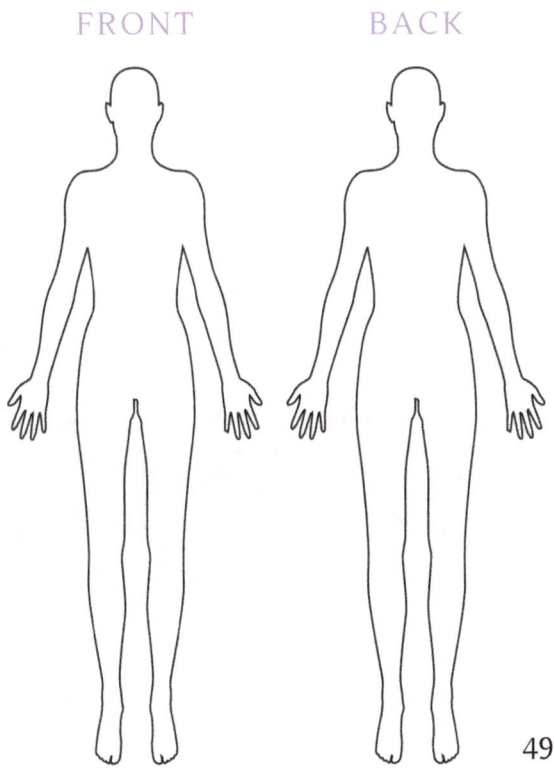

WHAT DO YOU NOTICE?

FRONT   BACK

17. Hold two opposites as equally divine, then uncover the expanse in the middle.

Do you hold strong likes and dislikes? What do you hate? What do you love? Recognize the value, the lesson, the purpose in all things. Understand the language of polarity, spectrum, and balance.

This exercise asks you to expand your worldview to have room for all truths. It asks you to hold these opposing truths in equal clarity and respects. It asks you for a willingness to exist in a world full of paradox and to fully accept it as it is.

This does not mean to give up on evolving always towards Love. It means to accept that the real story of it all is beyond your individual perception, much less comprehension. It asks you to have faith that ever-glowing consciousness will always heal shadow, even if you don't get to witness it.

This exercise reminds you that it is not for you to decide what is divine. It is for you to see glimpses of the divine in all things, from the lightest to the darkest. To see the wholeness in the middle.

WHAT DO YOU NOTICE?

FRONT   BACK

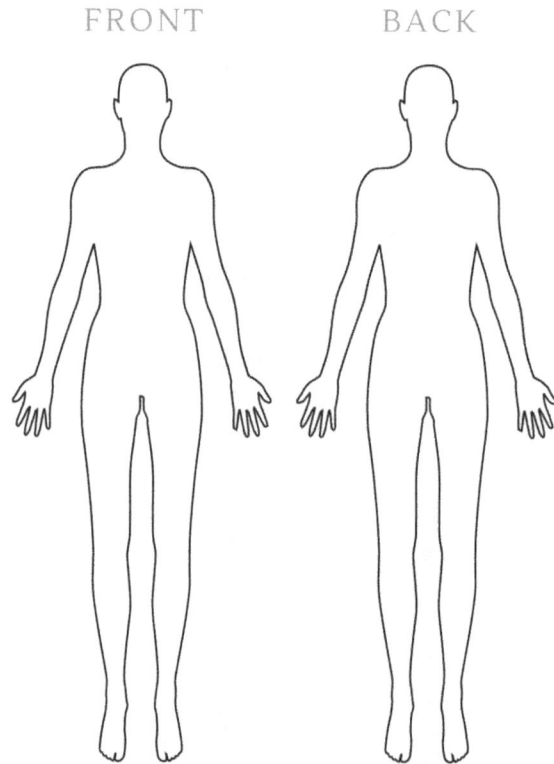

18. Gaze with loving care at an object,
real or imagined.
Let the warmth fill you.

Try this technique with many objects, each that you adore in a different way. Hold your favorite book or imagine your best friend, and allow that comfort to flood you from head to toe. Also try it with items that you don't adore. Gaze lovingly at a napkin, a random leaf, or a pen.

This is an exercise in harnessing the feeling of Love. Feel the tingling warmth expand out from your heart and stay with it as it moves through you, filling you completely. Connect deeply with the compassion and gratitude that come like heat from the glow of your loving kindness.

Try this even with objects or people that you dislike. Gaze lovingly at your least favorite food, a troublesome coworker, or a spider in the kitchen. How is your distaste transformed?

Try this exercise with all things and let gentleness, compassion, and a fundamental spiritual truth be revealed to you.

WHAT DO YOU NOTICE?

FRONT   BACK

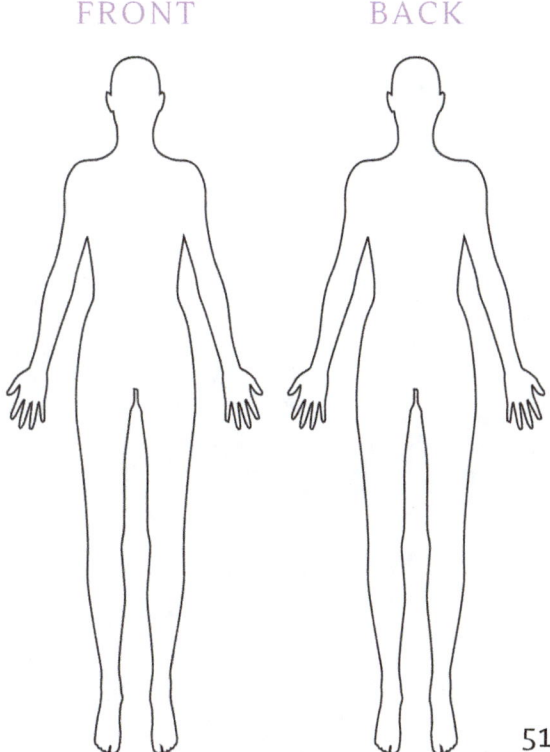

19. Rest only on your sit bones.
No hands, no feet.
Find balance there.

Creatively explore your body, finding its limits and then finding the balance there. Breathe deeply into this exploration and tune into the subtle sensations of the exercise. Listen closely to what they tell you about yourself.

As you perch on your sit bones, take a few deep sighs and guide your mind to take an even deeper notice of your body. If needed, look at an anatomy diagram to understand the mechanics and help you visualize your inner workings. There are subtle motions and sensations within your muscles, tendons, and ligaments. You can breathe, balance, and fine tune your inner understanding.

This meditation seeks to bring your wandering monkey mind into your body. It seeks to bring you back from the past, back from the future, and into this very present moment. To connect with your body's deep wisdom, balance your weight in all directions. Through this breathing and balancing, reconnect with your very existence on this planet.

WHAT DO YOU NOTICE?

FRONT   BACK

20.

When traveling as a passenger,
allow your body to rock with the motion.
In movement arises a still center.

Surrender to movement, like a child on a bouncing knee, like a leaf on the wind, dive deep into the sensation of being moved. Try closing your eyes and deeply feeling into the motion permeating your body.

What in you moves and what stays still? Does the movement unlock any of the tension you hold in your muscles? What happens if you will your body to relax and balance? Let your head, neck, and shoulders loosely roll as though dancing. Like a tree you sway, and maybe even bend, as reality moves in and around you.

Travel inward in this moving moment, centering yourself. Ground into the part of you that is observing the experience, the very seed of your consciousness that remains perfectly still. Like a gyroscope, your awareness balances at the center of your life. While the world continuously shifts, this omnipresent awareness remains a constant- in you as it does in all things.

WHAT DO YOU NOTICE?

FRONT   BACK

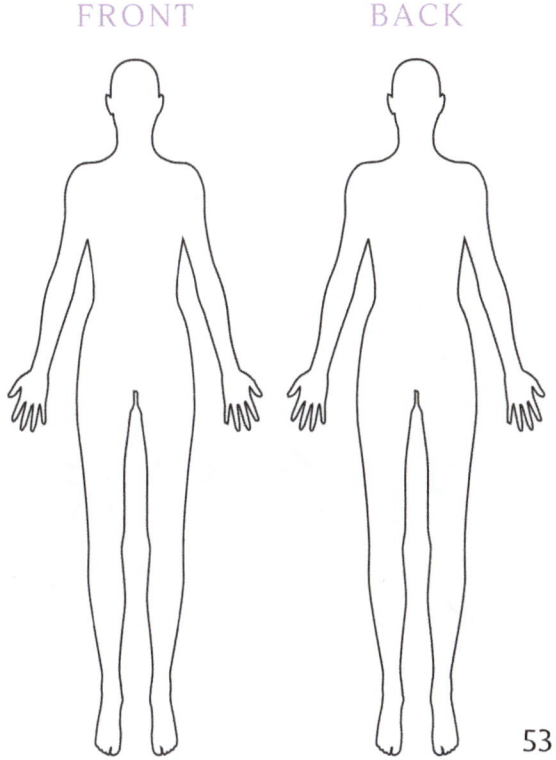

21. Find the pain in your body. Encompass it fully with loving, gentle awareness.

People spend so much time and energy avoiding pain. What happens when you are simply present to it instead? Meet pain at its front door with your most nurturing and soothing intentions. Unpack the separate sensations that we collectively call pain. Devote time to envisioning the anatomy of the place or places in your body where the discomfort exists. Hear your body's cries and offer them love.

Offer pain your deepest breath and nurturing awareness. Offer pain the light of divine healing and safety with each exhale, as though it were a small animal in need. As you do this exercise, find a deeper understanding of the subtlety of your body's language.

See the beautiful, extraordinary machine of a body that your consciousness is blessed to inhabit, even in pain. Like a spiritual engineer, use your inner tools to redirect your body's natural healing mechanisms like stem cells, oxytocin, and relaxation to soothe the pain. Find that you are so much more powerful than you realized.

WHAT DO YOU NOTICE?

FRONT   BACK

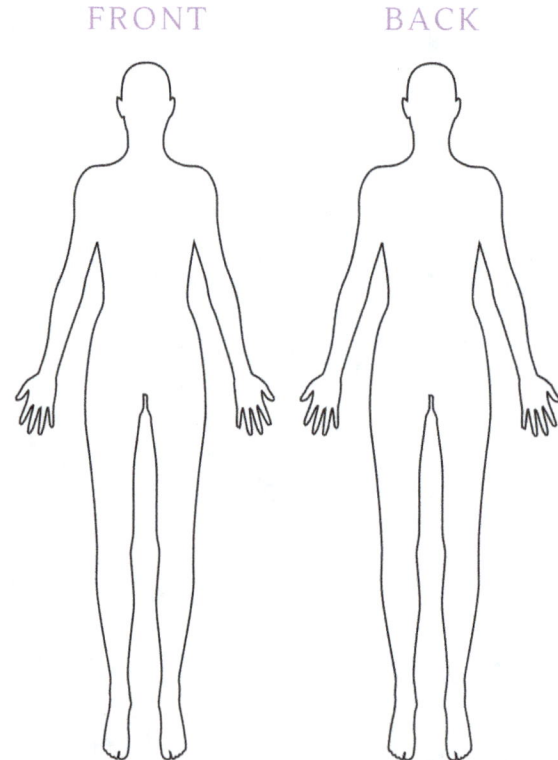

22. Recall your past as someone else's story. Let the disconnect bring you peace and understanding.

It is easy to get so immersed in the waters of your life story that you can drown in its many waves. You can forget how to hold your story lightly, how to float in such a heavy ship. To zoom out and see that story as belonging to someone else can reveal lessons and lifelines that were previously invisible.

This exercise is all about finding a perspective that you normally have to seek out from another person. A friend can see things in your story that you can't. Friends aren't attached to any outcome except your highest and greatest good, so they are more able to be honest about their interpretations.

For a change, become that friend for yourself. Tell yourself your story and really hear it as though it were the experience of another. Imagine being unbiased. What advice would you give? How much more clear does the picture become when you zoom out and take a fresh look? In this practice, see the bigger picture of it all and find peace.

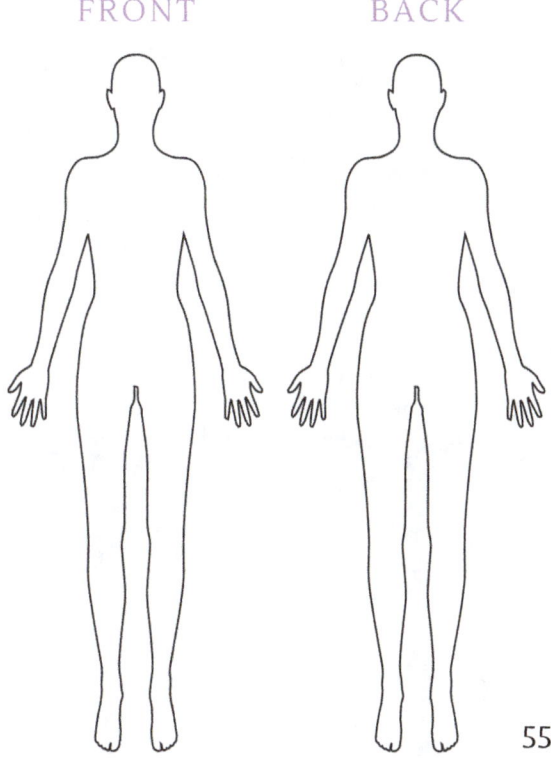

WHAT DO YOU NOTICE?

FRONT   BACK

55

23.
Experience an object with all your senses. When this overtakes you, forget the object and dissolve into consciousness.

Take a tea cup, a tree, or anything you can think and fully consider how each one of your senses perceives the object. Now forget the object itself and experience it just by the residual sensations.

Can random objects teach us about the nature of reality? When you connect each of your senses to an object, you connect with it in a deeper way. You may have never noticed the smell of a door or the sound of a book as the pages turn. You may have never taken the time to look deeply and study a speaker, or to feel the texture of pine needles on a tree.

At just the moment when the vast world of sensory experience overwhelms you, forget the object that started this journey and melt into pure presence. Stop trying to processes all the sensory input and simply observe as those sensations float around within you and slowly dissipate as that original object fades from your mind. In this moment sense something even deeper.

WHAT DO YOU NOTICE?

FRONT   BACK

24.
When filled with emotion, do not direct it outward.
Bring it inward to its source.
There, find that nothing controls you.

When an emotion arises, positive or negative, the tendency is to let it out, to express it through some sort of action. However, by holding and tracking an emotion to its root, you can then respond to whatever triggered the emotion from a place of grounded composure and reclaim your personal sovereignty. Was your annoyance rooted in exhaustion? Or your unhealthy attachment rooted in fear?

Once you have held and studied an emotion, you may find it easier to express those roots with more clarity and in a way that you won't later regret. And when you are in control of the way that you respond to the world you become much harder to manipulate. You take away the world's ability to provoke you.

This practice allows you to feel the full range of your emotional landscape and still be powerful, compassionate, and centered. It allows you to step out of mental stories and into a clarified truth, untainted by anyone or anything else. Your inner landscape becomes your freedom.

WHAT DO YOU NOTICE?

FRONT   BACK

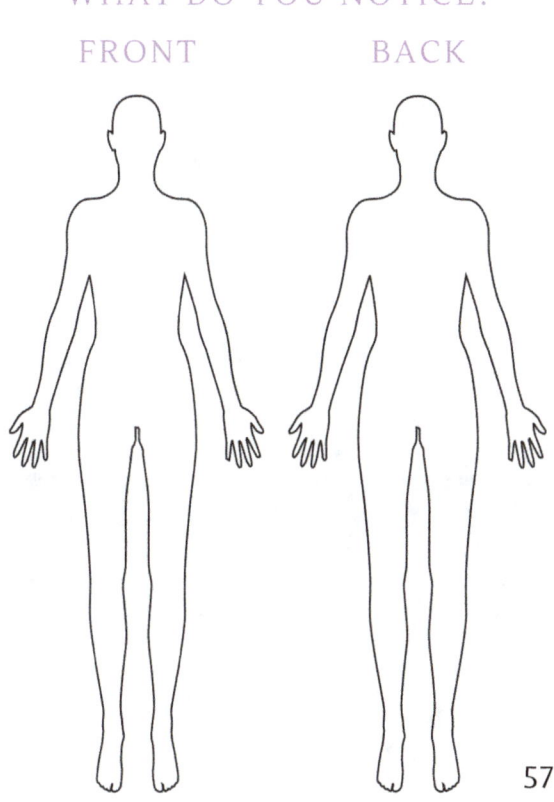

25.
As an action arises, suddenly stop.
In the sudden stop, awaken,
and the focus instead turns in.

Just before scratching an itch, before blurting out words, before reaching for a drink, before pressing play- stop. Pause for a moment to be present to yourself. What do you notice within? Anxiety? Clarity? Fear? Excitement? Whatever it is, just stop and be with your inner world. Does your action change after this momentary intermission?

This practice can teach you so much about yourself and the world around you. To stop and reflect at the moment before you take an action is a window into the subconscious patterns that can govern your life if you let them. Maybe you scratch because you're nervous, maybe you reach for a drink because you don't want to feel your heart hurt. Maybe you reach to call that friend because they genuinely make your heart glow.

Whatever layers you discover under the surface of your actions in this sudden stop, love them all. Meet them with curiosity, gentleness, and honesty. Evolve towards a wisdom that includes all of you.

WHAT DO YOU NOTICE?

FRONT   BACK

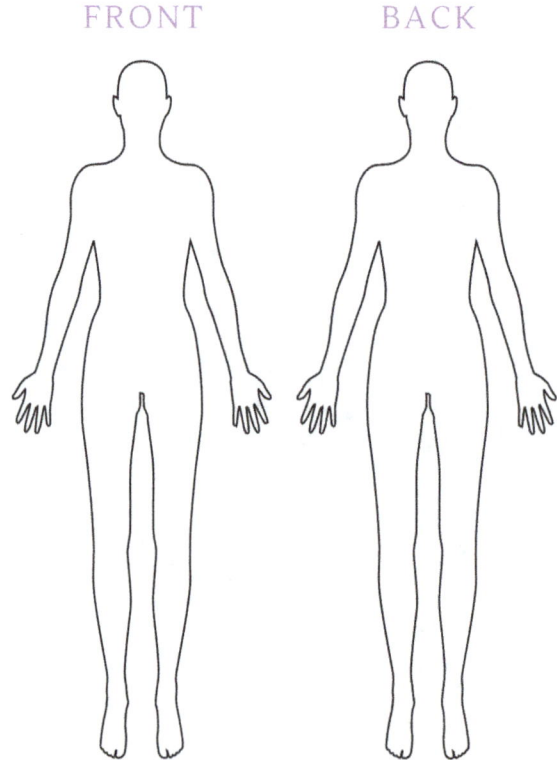

58

26. Study a desire. Then, without judgment, let it go.

Unpack your desire, trace it to its roots. Seek to understand it and to know what drives that desire. What hole in you is it seeking to fill? What does it look like for you to let go of that desire? A fight? A surrender? A relief? Is it possible that you will be just fine if that desire goes unfulfilled?

Try to offer understanding to your yearnings without writing a story around them. Is there something you constantly desire? All the more reason to dig deep within yourself to find out what hole you are trying to fill with that desire. Does the object of your desire distract you from pain? Does it save you from feeling lonely, depressed, or scared?

When you find this root, try simply letting go of the desire that sprouts from it. Hold no judgment and still, gently let it go with grace. Be honest with yourself about healing with therapy, support from loved ones, a journal, or grounding yourself in nature. Lay on the Earth and surrender to the winds. Realize all you need is already in you.

WHAT DO YOU NOTICE?

FRONT   BACK

27. Use your body until it becomes so tired
that you melt to the ground.
When totally melted, awaken.

Some already know this feeling well. Work all day in the garden, hike up a mountain, dance ecstatically, run, swim, play- until you simply have to stop and rest. Let yourself slip to the ground and melt totally into the Earth. Then feel the vibration in your body as you let your muscles give in to exhaustion.

When your body has finally come to an exhausted rest, what comes alive within you? Enter into the many subtle sensations in your bones and muscles. Find the gratitude of a body pushed to its maximum potential. Linger in the accomplishment and satisfaction of knowing your body did the most it could.

As more pieces of you come to rest, awaken to a non-desire, a lack of yearning, a fullness. Notice how rest feels different when you are genuinely physically exhausted. Witness in wonder, the miracle that is your body as it runs out of fuel and sputters to a stop.

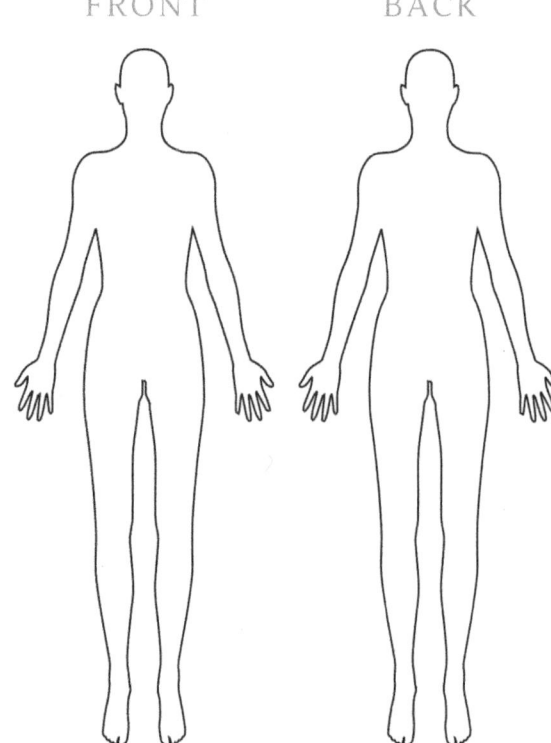

WHAT DO YOU NOTICE?

FRONT   BACK

28. Envision all the energy in your body draining from you like water from a vessel. Once empty, repose.

With each exhale feel yourself losing a bit more energy, as though you could use your willpower to completely drain yourself. Through this practice, soothe your anxiety, soothe your pain, soothe the human experience and find peace in being an empty vessel.

Like recreating the act of drifting to sleep, feel energy drain from your extremities inward. First your hands and your feet become empty of electricity. Then your legs and arms. What does this emptiness feel like as your energy seeps out? Out of which part of you does it drain? Let each breath drain a little more energy until you are still and completely clear.

Rest here in quietude, in a calm and tranquil body. As sparks of energy arise within your body and within your mind, gently exhale them back out. Return to a state of being that is separate from the stories of your life, that is void of any energy, that is defined by pure presence and potential.

WHAT DO YOU NOTICE?

FRONT   BACK

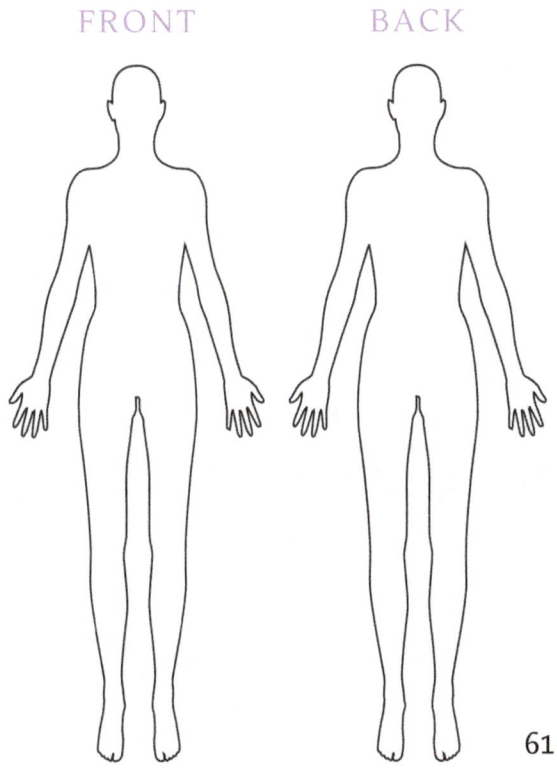

29. Transform desire into devotion.
In doing so, find liberation.

The nature of desire is that it always seeks to fill some void within. Whatever the object is, food, clothes, or sex- desire wants attachment. It seeks to grab the object or experience and to never let it go. Desire never wants the pleasure to end.

This creates suffering in two ways. First, because all things are impermanent, there will be sorrow. The meal will end, the sex will end, the clothing will go out of style. Eventually, you will lose it all. The second suffering is that these things don't actually fill the void within. Once you acquire the object of desire, suddenly a new one arises and you continue to to be unfulfilled. You remain hungry.

Instead take that yearning energy and devote it to your highest and greatest good or to some cause greater than your fleeting cravings. This will free you from the misery those desires create. Devote yourself to divine acts of kindness, devote yourself to senseless acts of beauty, devote yourself to growth, devote yourself to sacred partnership. In this devotion you will become free.

WHAT DO YOU NOTICE?

FRONT   BACK

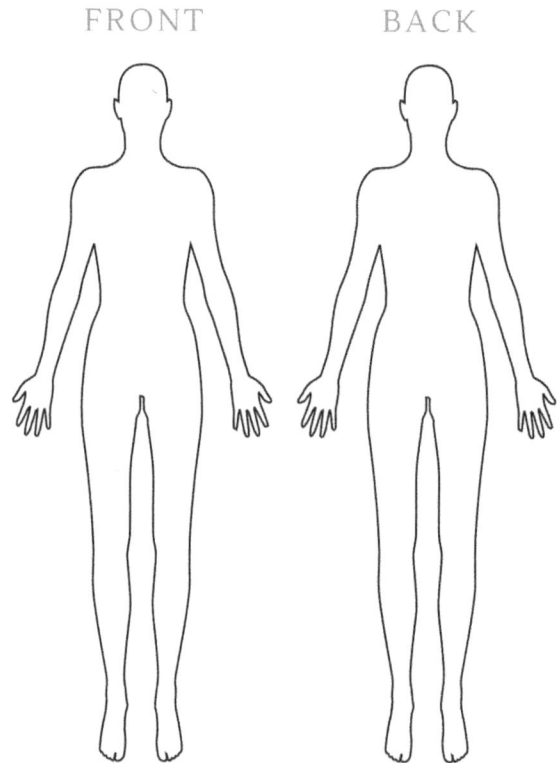

30.

Let the eyelids fall like curtains.
Invite your awareness
to explore your vast interior world.

Like peacefully closing yourself in a darkened room, open to your reflective imagination, or interoception, with this meditation. Take the time to notice all that happens in the moonless caverns of your body when you commit your awareness to explore its mysterious interior realms.

With deep expanding breaths, become aware of both the most noticeable and the most subtle sensations in your body. As you continue to breathe deeply into your interoception, allow your imagination to run wild and give visualizations to this inner experience. Study how your breath and observation affect this sweeping inner realm of emotions and thoughts.

Imagine yourself walking through a forest of you, turning over stones and peeking into bushes. Swim through your ocean, crawl in your caves, and meet creatures. Connect to your inner world with curiosity, acceptance, and love to better know the divine limitless being that you are.

WHAT DO YOU NOTICE?

FRONT   BACK

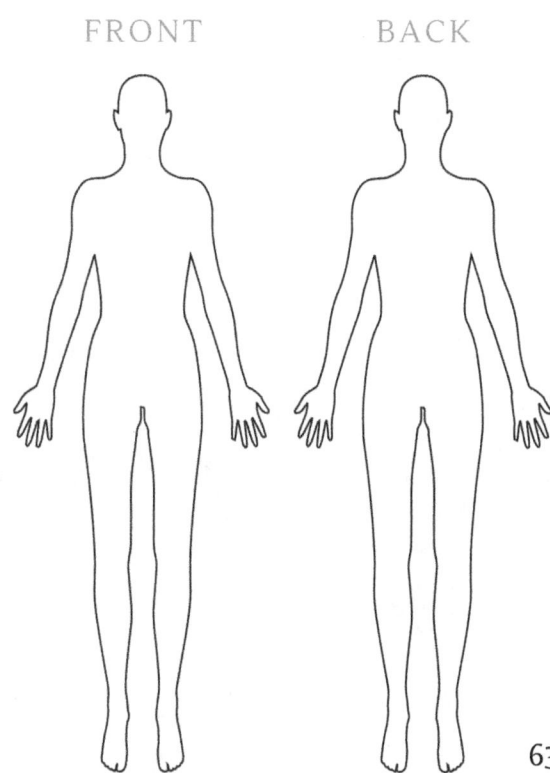

31. Gaze upon an object without seeing its parts. Absorb its undivided wholeness.

Explore what it means to see an object as a whole, as a singular entity. Instead of trees, see a forest. Instead of cars, see a parking lot. Instead of bricks, see a wall. Instead of flaws or beauty, see a whole person. Instead of individuals, see all of humanity as undivided. All life itself as undivided.

We create so much pain for ourselves and others when we see things and people as separate from one another. We limit the truth we can experience when we break the world into its pieces and its parts. We miss the inherent connections between all things and so we miss the whole picture.

This technique seeks to instill a wider perspective, a shift in worldview such that it becomes easier to digest all truths in their wholeness. A shift to a view that has room for all things, from the smallest seed to the most vast rainforest that contains it. From the briefest thought to the whole being that pondered it. All things have a greater whole when you let yourself see it.

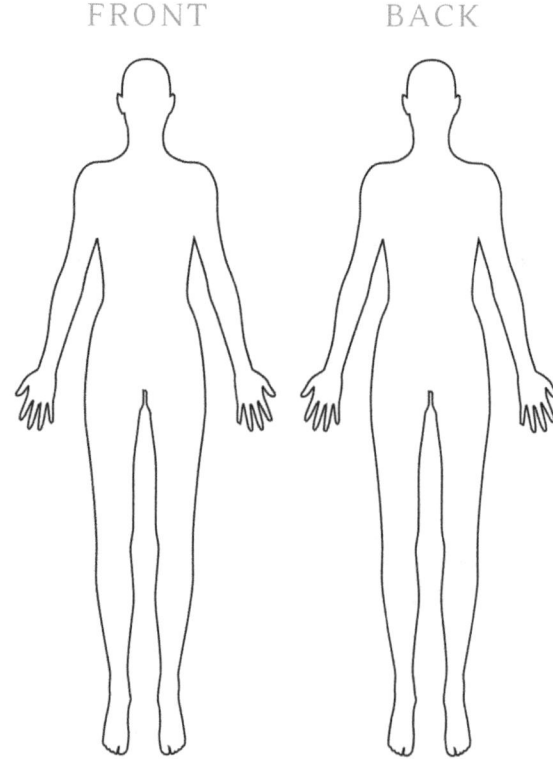

WHAT DO YOU NOTICE?

FRONT   BACK

32. Imagine seeing a person or object as though taking in a completely new experience.

There is a certain energetic quality to experiencing something new. A freshness, a curiosity, an openness that ceases to exist when we feel that a person or an object is known. Recreate and reconnect with the mystery of newness by simply choosing to see something anew.

As you gaze at a familiar person or well known item, imagine that you could erase all your associated memories. Take a deep breath, blink your eyes, and take it all in as though for the first time. See a lover like you saw them on the day you met. Walk into your home as though you've never seen it. Study the branches of a thick, old tree like you were an extraterrestrial being visiting Earth for the first time.

Notice what is revealed to you as you experiment with this technique. How many qualities have you overlooked in people and things that you know well? Become aware of how true perception is limited by the histories we write.

WHAT DO YOU NOTICE?

FRONT   BACK

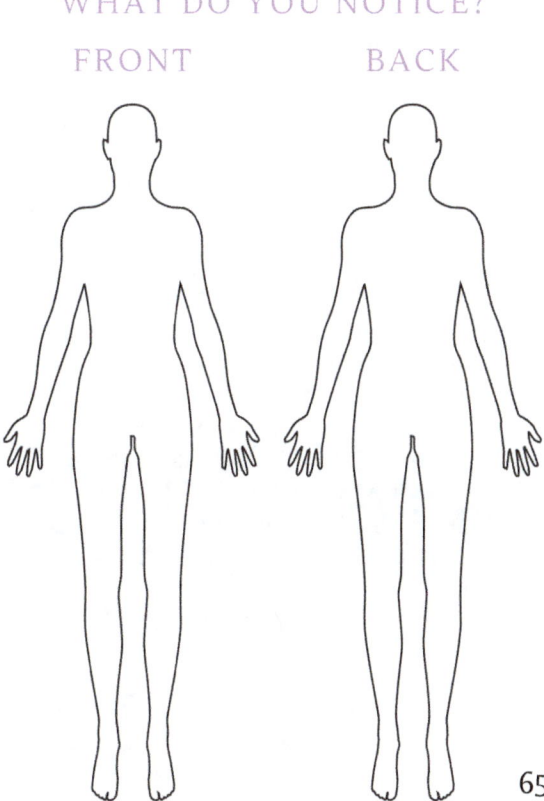

65

33. Gaze deeply into the endless expanse of the sky, and beyond into infinity.

It can be easy to forget about the vast wonders that dwell outside the thin veil of Earth's atmosphere. As you gaze out at the sky, contemplate the infinite space that lies beyond our little planet.

Consider the fabric of the cosmos reaching out to an endless space. With gentleness, allow your mind to melt around this abstract concept, all while staring out and through the edges of the planet. Ponder the mysteries there, the science we have yet to learn, the realities that humans simply can't perceive.

Rather than a sense of concern about how small and insignificant you are, feel yourself perfectly nestled into this vast wonderland. Reflect on all that came together in that expanse of the cosmos to make YOU. Know that same mysterious serendipity is still supporting you on your journey to live fully, to live with love, and to live with wonder. Gaze out and see your own infinite potential.

WHAT DO YOU NOTICE?

FRONT   BACK

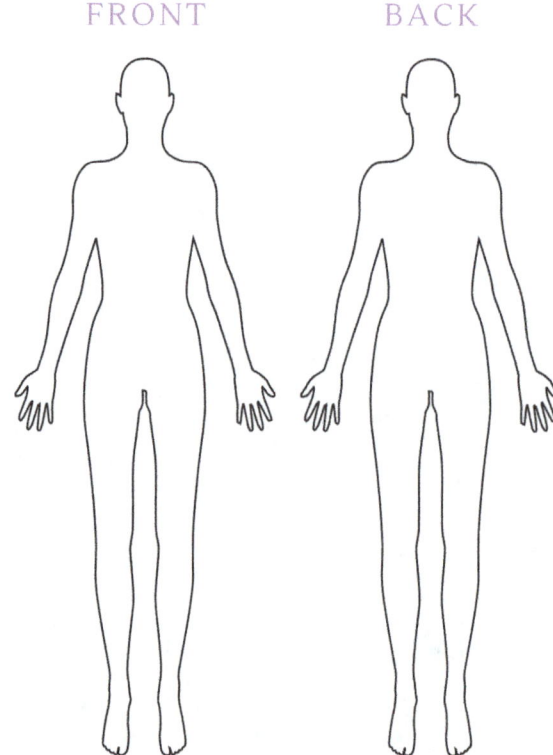

34. Fully experience a moment of awakening
when sitting with a teacher.
Let it infuse with your whole being.

Find a spiritual guide or teacher that you connect with and respect. In your studies with this person, you will likely have an experience of awakening to deep, reverent truths. When this occurs, linger in the feeling that permeates your body and spirit. Rest in the expansiveness and replenishment of your spiritual education.

This technique centers around capturing moments of enlightenment, or shaktipatas, as you learn sacred tools, techniques, and concepts. This is for times that you feel your consciousness piercing the veil of the illusions created as your mind processes and defines reality- for the times when you see beyond the mundane stories of daily life.

Deeply consider how this awakening feels on all levels of your being. When the veil is lifted, how does your mind respond? How does your body connect to this? Feel it in your skin and in your very bones. Feel sacred truths expand from your heart to fill you and infuse you with their wisdom.

WHAT DO YOU NOTICE?

FRONT   BACK

67

35. When staring into a deep hole, awaken to the miracle of existence.

This will work with any deep hole, well, ice core, mineshaft, or even cave. As you let your eyes fall down into the darkness, imagine it as a mere pin prick into the surface of the Earth. Wonder at how small you are in the grand scale. Visualize how many times you could stand on your own head to reach the same height as this hole.

Think of the minuscule size of each particle of soil and rock making up the walls of the hole. In awe, think of each atom within each of those particles. As small as humans are, we are also equally giant in this paradoxical reality.

Even more so, let your mind linger in the empty space of the hole as you replicate that openness in your own being. Merge with depth and clarity in a space that is so large from one perspective and so small from another. Allow a miraculous truth sink in.

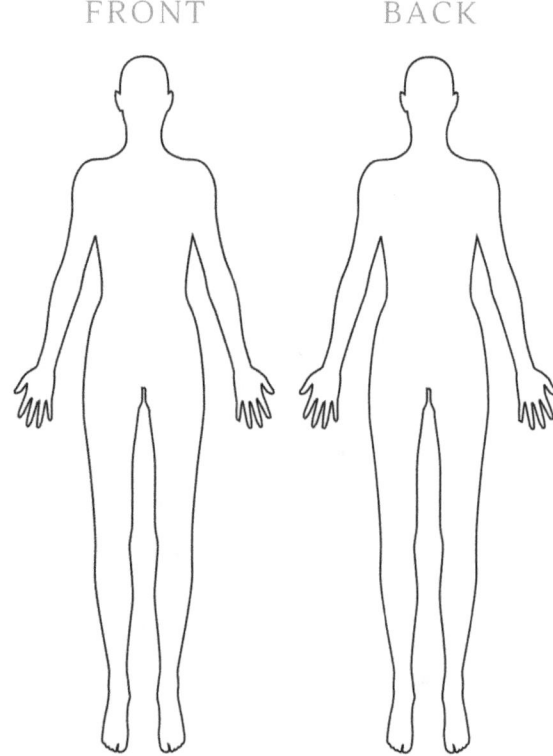

WHAT DO YOU NOTICE?

FRONT   BACK

36.

Focus on an item. Then close your eyes, seeing it's image. Then let the image go, and there it is- pure perception.

Consider an object that brings you deep comfort and peace. Perhaps it is too big to carry with you, or maybe it fits snugly in your pocket. Gaze at the object and take in all of its sensory aspects. Notice its smell, its texture, its shape, and its color. Then close your eyes and feel this vivid experience filling your mind's eye.

Once your eyes are closed, hold your connection to the image and feel it in your heart. Once you let the image in your head go, reach out in your consciousness for the simplest essence of this object, its core feeling. Hold that sensation in your body. Remember it in your heart.

If you can clearly connect with the image or essence of an item in your mind's eye, then you can use it as a tool to support your spiritual and emotional health. Try this meditation with a range of objects, real and imagined. Connect with the pure perception of all that surrounds you and find that any essence is always within your reach.

WHAT DO YOU NOTICE?

FRONT   BACK

69

37. Notice the letters in words. Notice the sound of letters. Notice the feeling of sounds. Then notice something beyond.

Do you ever say a word so many times that it begins to sound strange coming out, that it suddenly loses all meaning? That is one way to stumble into this revealing, mystical meditation.

Another way is to pick a word, any word that you wish to be a mantra. Speak the word and notice each letter, their shapes, and the way they fit next to each other. Sound out each letter, giving deep consideration as its vibration leaves your lips.

Feel the sounds in each letter as they roll through your mouth and vibrate in your body. Does "M" vibrate deep into your belly? Does "T" linger higher in your body? What of the letter "Z"?

As you do this, become aware of the unique oscillations of sounds within you. Reflect on the countless ancestors whose voices came together to create the words and letters you now speak. Reflect on the idea that reality itself is spoken into existence by a soundless sound.

WHAT DO YOU NOTICE?

FRONT   BACK

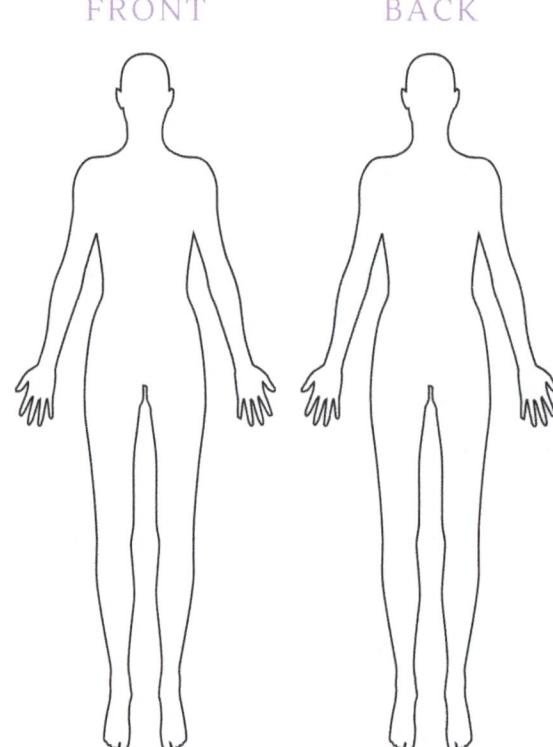

70

38.

Feel the way that sounds,
loud or quiet, encircle you.
Find the center.

Wherever you are, close your eyes and visualize the sounds you hear wrapping around your body. What if you could see the concentric waves as they move through the air, passing around and enveloping obstacles like water?

Feel the sound encircling you, as though its waves could enclose your whole being in an embrace. How far do they permeate into your body? Feel sound reaching a deep place within you and imagine these undulations converging around a central point in your inner world. What is this center?

Notice subtle changes in your perception when you allow hearing to encompass all your other senses. Try this technique with a variety of unique sounds in order to understand it in increasingly subtle ways. The songs of nature, the cadence of a lover's voice, the whir of traffic, a quiet night, or ocean waves. Notice how each of these encircle you in their own singular frequency. Then see again the unchanging center within you where they meet.

WHAT DO YOU NOTICE?

FRONT   BACK

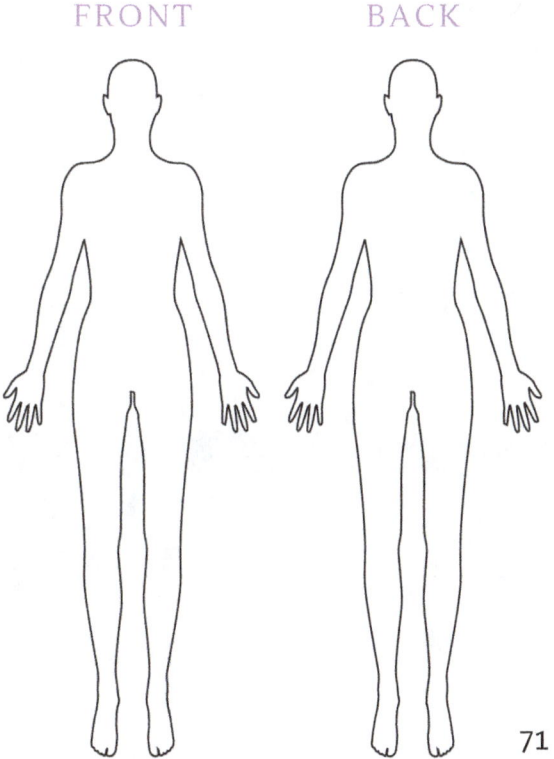

71

39. Articulate a sound. Feel it move through you until you and the sound share the same vibration.

Sound is one of the great movers of stagnant energy that builds up in the body over time. Tune into whatever sound your spirit needs in any given moment and unlock the true effectiveness of this technique. What sound does your body desire to make right now, in this moment? Take a deep breath in and see what comes out when you exhale.

First, feel the sound vibrating in your heart, your throat, and your belly. Continue vocalizing until you feel the vibration reach into every corner of your body, from your toes to your crown. Make this noise until its frequency is so strong that it permeates and merges with you on all levels.

Once you have infused with the vocalization, linger there in its resonance. Sink deeper and deeper into the message and the lesson of the sound as it vibrates your truth into existence. Each time you practice, uncover a new sacred truth about yourself and the world. What do you notice in your body before this practice? And after?

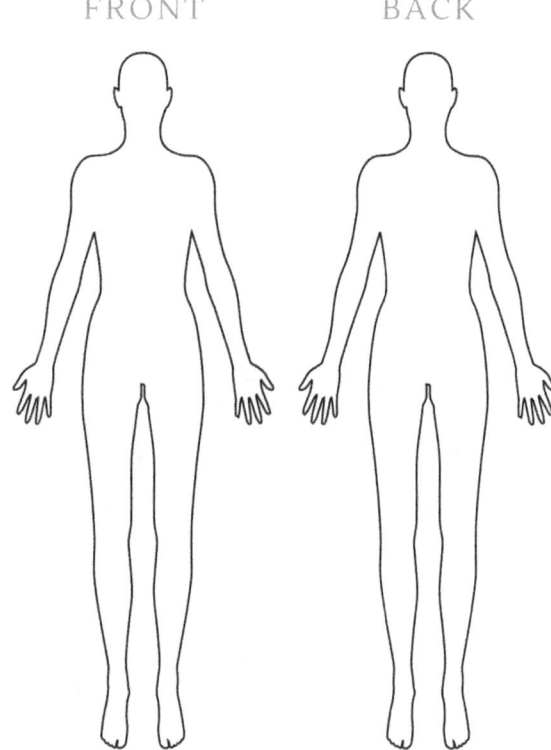

WHAT DO YOU NOTICE?

FRONT   BACK

40. Let your awareness embrace a sound
as it gets closer to you,
and again as it gets farther away.

This practice encourages you to find the mystical in the mundane. Tune into the sounds around you, whether it's wind in the trees, traffic on a road, a train on tracks, an approaching plane, or the sounds of taking a run. There you will find an intersection of the science and the lived experience of moving sound.

Visualize the sound waves rippling towards you through space and time. As they approach you, the wave shortens and the pitch increases until it reaches its true sound. As it moves away, you receive the sound waves as they are stretching out, lowering the pitch you hear. It is basic science and also a tiny window to the waving nature of reality.

Consider this fascinating, aspect of the world and wonder at the dynamic nature of it all. Understand that this is also the nature of light, of water, of our very thoughts. Each time you hear a sound approach from afar, let your consciousness ride the wave of existence.

WHAT DO YOU NOTICE?

FRONT   BACK

41. Allow the many sounds of a stringed instrument
to enter you as one.
Such is the nature of reality.

Let the harmonizing vibrations of a guitar, a sitar, a violin, or any stringed instrument flood into your experience of reality. Feel the unique, but unified sounds radiate through every inch of your being. Envision the cells in your body resonating with the music, creating goosebumps and raising hairs.

Ponder the motion of each string when plucked into a wave, whipping at the surrounding air and rippling out through space and time into your ears. Picture this motion again and again for each string- waves through the air, overlapping concentric circles that miraculously blend together in your ear to create the gentle caress of a soft violin.

Now take the leap and understand that all existence works in this way. Light, electricity, magnetism, sound, thoughts, even the pressure waves from your heart, all come together to harmonize into one ever moving symphony of reality.

WHAT DO YOU NOTICE?

FRONT   BACK

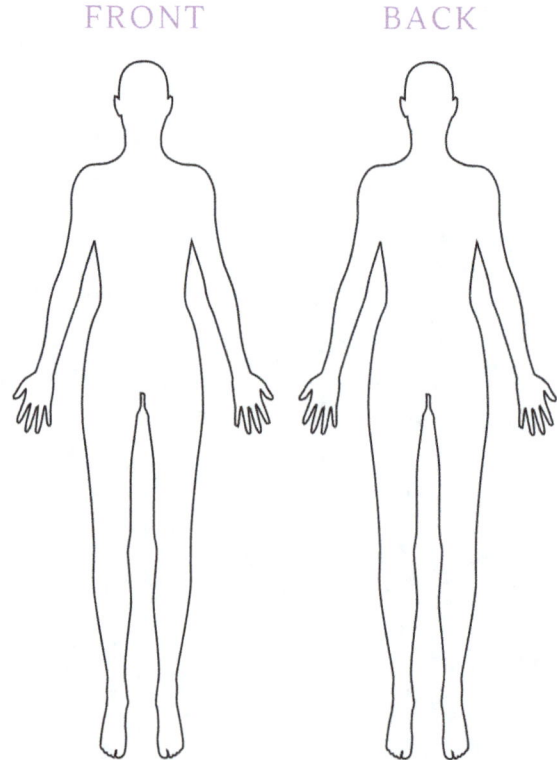

42. Make a sound that slowly gets quieter.
As it quiets, see the feeling behind the sound.
See yourself in the feeling.

Shout! Hummm, groan, laugh, cry, sing- make whatever sound wants to come out at this very moment. Be fully present to it as it starts and as it fades slowly from your vocal chords. Draw out the noise as long as you can and let it dissolve slowly from your lips with your breath.

Bring your awareness to the way the sound vibrates in your body. Feel it in your throat, your chest, and your whole head. Feel what inside you, under the vibration, drove this sound to come out. Notice without judgement the thought or emotion sparked this noise- and when you find it, linger there.

When your mind connects to the root of the sound, visualize it. How do you see your peace, your anger, your excitement? In tracking your vocalizations, notice how something as simple as a sound can reflect your honest truth back to you in a new light. Meet yourself here, in the fleeting emanations of the heart, ebbing and flowing with feeling and sound.

WHAT DO YOU NOTICE?

FRONT   BACK

75

43.

Bring awareness to the middle of your tongue as the sound of your breath passes effortlessly over its surface.

As though your mind's eye were a camera, zoom your focus into this sacred spot in the middle of your tongue. As pranic life force, or air, flows both in and out of your body, feel the electricity awaken here in your mouth. Be mindful not to strain as you do this exercise. Relax your jaw, your lips, your whole body, and especially your tongue. Then notice.

Where else is electricity awakening in your body as you do this? Understand that this spot on your tongue is in alignment with Sushumna, the channel of energy that passes through the very center of your body. This divine, electric channel is encased in a double helix of masculine and feminine energy flows. The trio of power lines can reset any misalignment within you when you use your breath, focus, and visualization to tap in.

The center of the tongue is one of many access points to bring in the healing power of breath and to unlock your true, peaceful, expansive nature. Linger in this exercise, let it rejuvenate you.

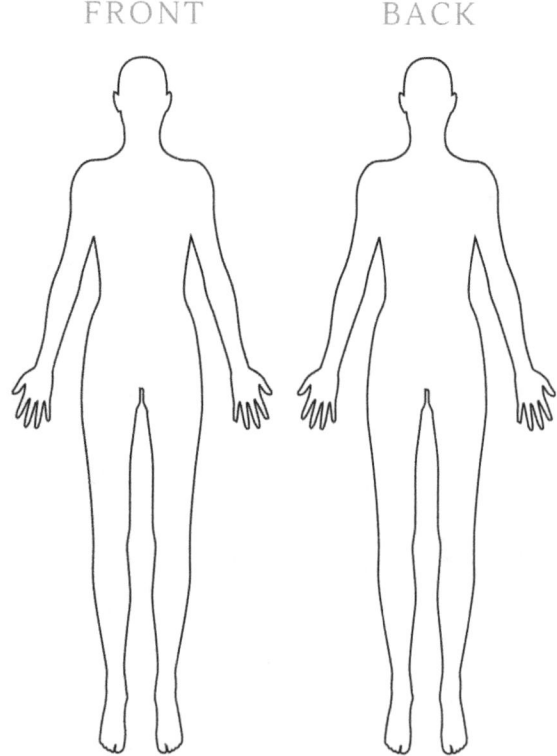

WHAT DO YOU NOTICE?

FRONT   BACK

44. Become aware of the most quiet and subtle of sounds, therein finding soundlessness.

Wherever you are, listen closely. Maybe start with the loudest sound you can hear, right now, in this moment. In your mind, track that sound to its source and then find the next loudest sound. Do this until you start listening to the quietest sound you can hear. Let your ears come alive with sensitivity as you tune deeply into your environment.

This practice invites you to enhance your awareness of the world around you. As you connect into the quietest sound you connect into everything else that is subtle too. All your other senses awaken. You can see beyond seeing, hear beyond earshot, even perceive the imperceptible.

Notice what this does to your perception of the space around you. Notice that your breath is sometimes the loudest noise you hear and, conversely, sometimes it is the quietest sound of all. Become aware of the subtlest sound, and then of a mystical something beyond.

WHAT DO YOU NOTICE?

FRONT   BACK

45. Silently express "ahhhh" as a mantra. Suddenly, feel yourself let go.

This technique will meet you wherever you find yourself. The mantra may start out as a quick breath, with an inhale and a brief "ah" of an exhale. Repeat it. Stretch it out, so that the silent ahhhh lengthens, filling the space of a long exhale.

Notice what happens to the tension in your jaw, your chest, your shoulders, your face, and your whole body as you suddenly let go and melt deeper into this silent practice. Once or twice, try expressing the letters out loud just to feel it move through your chest, neck, and head. But return again to the noiseless expression of relief.

Envision this movement of breath and soundless sound as a cool breeze grazing over you heart, gently stirring up all that is stagnant within you, spilling out tension and inhaling peace. Allow your muscles and spirit to let go of the burdens you carry as you exhale in a quiet relief. Consider how something so quiet can be so strong.

WHAT DO YOU NOTICE?

FRONT   BACK

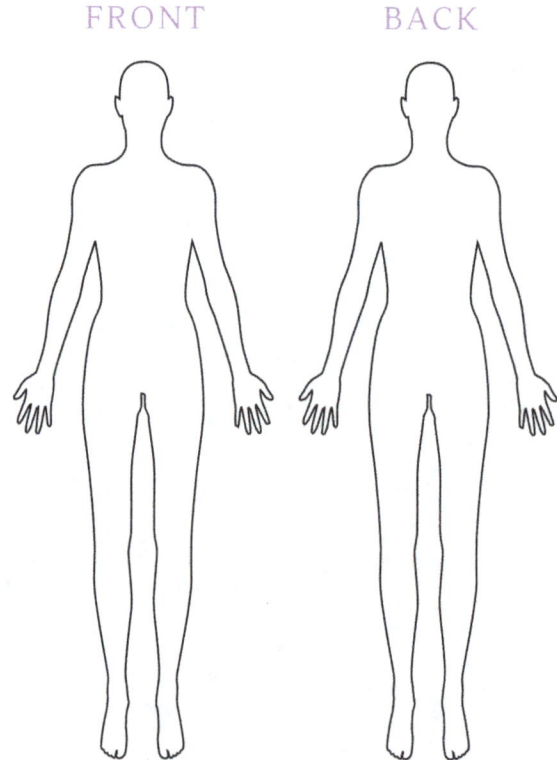

46. Plug your ears, squeeze your root, enter fully into the sound created throughout your body.

Closing off your experience of perception in this way is akin to submerging yourself underwater. In this case, the water is the quiet void of your inner world. When you close your ears and squeeze your pelvic floor you are diving into the deep waters of your self to discover a respite from the sounds of your thoughts and the outside world.

Instead you will find a new noiseless noise, one that emanates from your head and expands to fill you. Take close notice of the vibration that awakens within you when you explore this practice. Feel it soak into your whole being from head to toe as you breathe deeply and keep your focus inward.

Let the frequency of pulsing stillness connect you to something more ethereal, more ephemeral. As though you could match the vibration of the Earth beneath your feet, the movement of an ocean, or the passing of the stars overhead- enter into the sanctuary of your body's natural hum.

WHAT DO YOU NOTICE?

FRONT   BACK

47. Repeat your name like the prayer that it is.

Say your name. Say it slowly. Say it quickly. Sound it out and feel the vibration, the essence, and the character of the word. Speak your own name like it brings you to life! Again and again, say it like it calls back all the pieces of yourself that you've left behind over the years.

Say your name and feel it in your mouth. Pronounce it again and feel it vibrate out into the world like ripples in a pond. Say it as one of the Divine's infinite names. Repeat your own name and feel more full of love each time. This practice can at once empower you as an expansive creation of the divine cosmos while also nestling you into your tiny home amongst the vast pantheon of souls.

Praying your name can reveal your creative purpose in this life. It can water and fertilize the seed of your potential. Its ancestral vibration can awaken and support you in your evolution. Say your name and find your home within it.

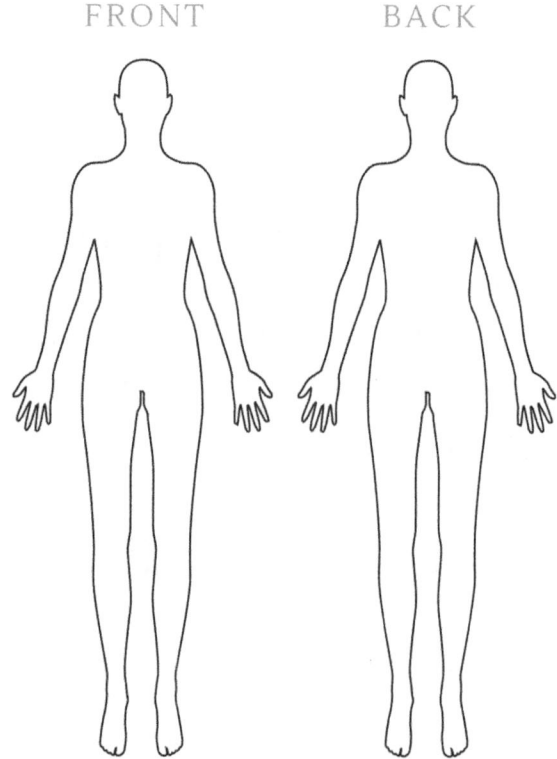

WHAT DO YOU NOTICE?

FRONT   BACK

48. Be fully present to the experience of sexual pleasure without orgasm.

What shifts in life when you remove goals and savor each moment for it's own sake? This technique is one of the central teachings that westerners have taken from the wealth of tantric wisdom. It opens up a door to a realm where sexuality is an expression of divine life force. It is a devoted practice of lovingly sitting with and studying pleasure.

Instead of obeying desire that rushes to an explosive release, use breath, intention, and visualization to simultaneously contain and expand the sensation of pleasure. Let it fill your whole being from head to toe. Linger in the melting and allow the experience to heal you, to teach you, and to reveal a new state of being to you.

From this new evolved, luscious state of being you can meet and bathe in your higher self, in a devotional truth where pleasure coexists with meaning and purpose. Discover the compassion, wisdom, and peace of turning desire inward.

WHAT DO YOU NOTICE?

FRONT   BACK

49.

**Like a breeze shakes the flowers,
let sexual pleasure shake you
into total surrender.**

When you have learned to let the experience of pleasure linger in your body instead of rushing to release it, you may begin to notice a vibration that echos through your muscles. It could begin in your hands, your feet, or your thighs. And it may come on strong and rumble through your whole body.

Whenever this occurs, try allowing the shaking to overtake you. You may want to stop the shaking for fear of embarrassment, but instead surrender to it as a celebration of sensual movement. Surrender to the flow of energy coursing through you, open yourself to the release of long stagnant energies held in your muscles.

Breathe deeply into this vibrating, pulsing electricity as it reaches every corner of your body. Breathe deeply and allow the sublimation to run its course, trusting in its ability to heal and soothe you in all places. When the shaking finally subsides, linger in the ultimate stillness, the ultimate melting peace.

WHAT DO YOU NOTICE?

FRONT   BACK

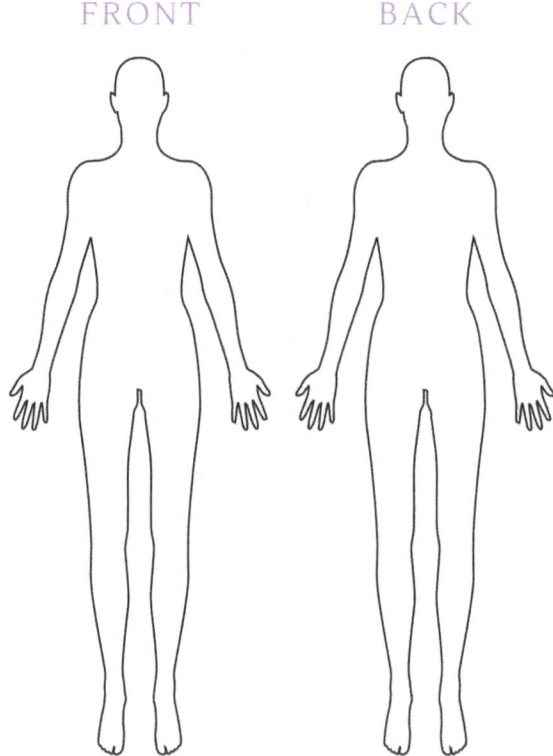

Sexuality is arguably the most potent energy in the body. This practice is an essential tool for learning about its complex nature. Understand that sexual energy itself is neither good nor bad. That distinction comes from whether we express the shadow side or the light side of the given energy.

The shadow side of sexuality can be one of the world's darkest and, conversely, its light has the power to connect you to the most divine states of being. Are your intentions clean and clear or have they been muddied by desire? Find the clear intentions by discovering yourself through devotion.

Get comfortable and create ceremony in your own way- play music, light a burning bundle, and drop in. Breathe slowly, turn your focus inward, and visualize pleasure as your hands gently explore your body without any goal. Observe how your breath affects your sensations, how it grows the seed of pleasure within you. Stay connected to this seed and to your breath as you guide pleasure up through your body. Bring it from root to crown and awaken to its true nature.

WHAT DO YOU NOTICE?

FRONT   BACK

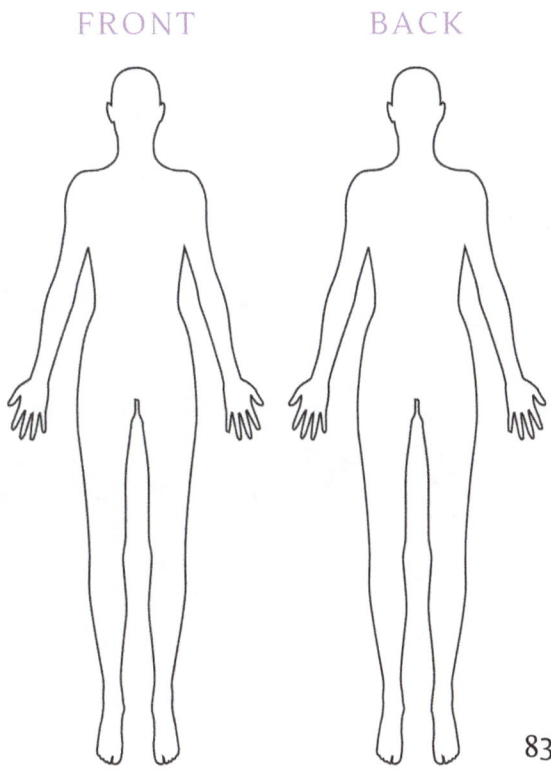

83

51.

In a moment of pure joy,
enter fully into the sensation.
Merge with the delight, let it encompass all of you.

Each person knows experiences of pure bliss, even if only for the briefest of moments. There is a sensation that overcomes all of your senses. Your body warms and the central observer in you comes fully alive and present. This exercise asks you to lean into that state of being. Become aware of your whole body and its exalted lightness.

These heightened times of pure joy are meant to be savored and fully embodied. They are a gift to you and like any gift you love, take the time to cherish it. Hold it close to your heart so that the memory of this precious moment is close by when you need to remember the beauty of the world.

Start remembering beauty by fully experiencing it when it is actually happening. Let all of your senses take note of joy. Embrace sounds you hear, the smells, the sights, the feeling on your skin, and even the taste in your mouth. Embrace them all so that you can remember with your whole body, so that feeling is always just a breath away.

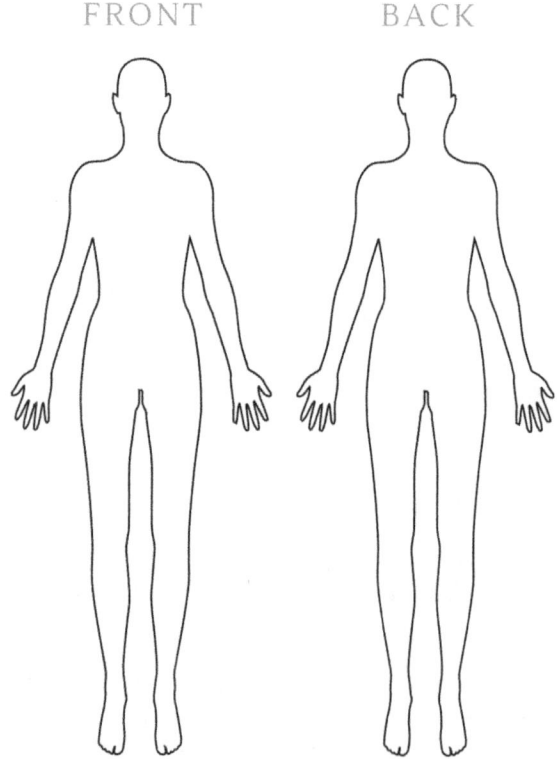

WHAT DO YOU NOTICE?

FRONT   BACK

52. Deeply savor and appreciate each bite of food and each sip of drink. Experience it as your whole being.

It is too easy to rush through meals, to not fully chew each bite, much less to take the time to deeply savor the sensations that occur in your mouth, eyes, ears, and nose. Open yourself to a new way of experiencing the present moment through your senses.

As you eat, take in the appearance of your meal. Is it beautiful? Odd looking? Notice the feeling in your mouth. Is it soft or crunchy? Can you smell it? How does your nose react? Try considering the most obvious sense last. Taste the food you just put in your body and study the layers of flavor. Visualize it as it moves down into your stomach. Where else in your body can you feel this meal? Become aware of subtle sensations through out your whole being.

When you give this much presence and attention to the act of eating you can connect with the gift of food in a more meaningful way. You can connect with the mundane miracle of rejuvenation through nourishment.

WHAT DO YOU NOTICE?

FRONT   BACK

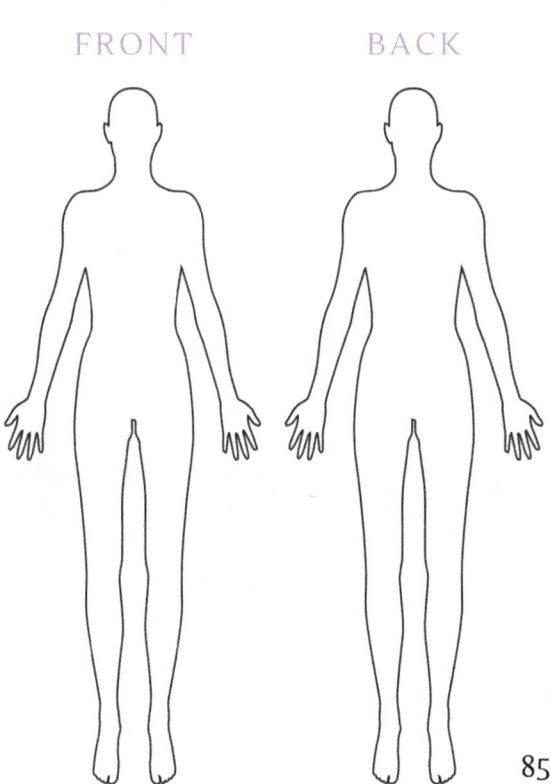

53. In any activity, awaken to the ever-glowing light of your own consciousness.

It is always there, always. Reflect on that spark of awareness that is continually perceiving from within you. Do you feel connected to your inner observer? Do you confuse it with your inner critic or your inner daydreamer?

Awaken to your own ever-present consciousness by stepping out of the narrated story of your life and into the position of the observer. The classical tantric worldview sees all existence as a relationship between the observer, the observed, and the act of observing. Ponder this.

The part of you that observes is not attached to the story. Find this part that watches and whispers simple divine truths. You'll recognize your own ever-glowing consciousness by its gentle curiosity, by its honest and clear perspective, by the bliss you feel when connected to it. This part of you is beyond the stories you tell. At any point you can simply pause and awaken to this flame of awareness, awaken to the warm glow of its truth.

WHAT DO YOU NOTICE?

FRONT   BACK

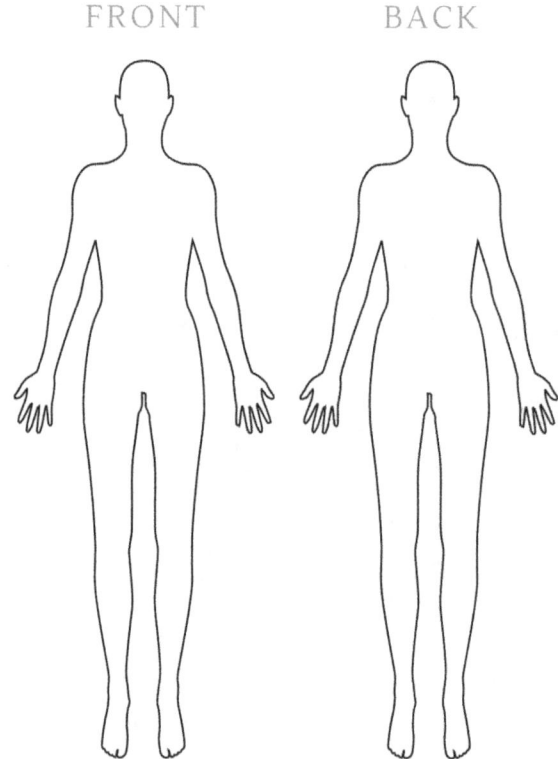

54. When feeling fulfilled, contented, or satisfied, melt into the fullness with your whole being.

When you find yourself in a place of contentment, linger in it. Notice your whole being, from head to toe and how each part of you responds to deep satisfaction. Where in your body do you feel fulfilled and what does it feel like?

People spend so much time desiring one thing or another. It is essential to take time to soak up the moments when you feel no desire at all, the moments when you are completely at peace. These times teach your whole body how to exist in a state of contentment. Create a memory of this feeling, this state of mind, this fullness.

The real practice of this meditation is to discover the difference between true contentment and the fleeting happiness of attaining a superficial desire. When truly fulfilled, you aren't craving more, you aren't reaching for the next thing. Let this practice hone what genuinely brings you to a place of fulfillment. Let it show you a path to lasting peace.

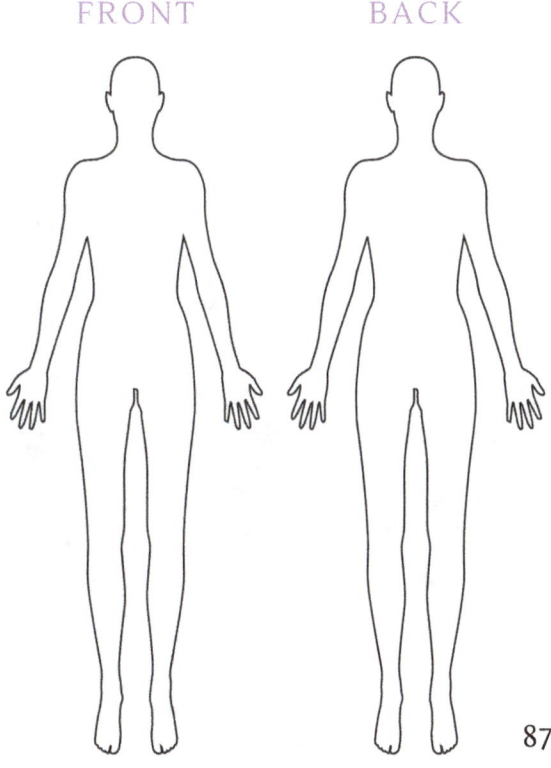

WHAT DO YOU NOTICE?

FRONT   BACK

55. Take close notice of the moment before falling asleep.
The space between reveals pure consciousness.

When falling asleep, the mind often meanders unconsciously through its thoughts until drifting off into the realm of dreams. Sometimes this wandering is anxious while at other times it is quite peaceful, but it is almost always aimless and lacking intention.

This technique invites you to explore the magic of this subtle transition we make each night between wakefulness and rest. To create intention around sleep, consider repeating a prayer or a mantra that is close to your heart. As you repeat this saying in your mind, create a gentle visual to accompany it. Perhaps walk yourself through a forest or roll around on a sandy beach. Whatever feels meaningful to you is perfect.

Breathe deeply in your belly and closely observe as the muscles in your body begin to shut down and rest. Lightly watch as your consciousness slips out and into its nightly journey, subtly revealing your true ethereal nature.

WHAT DO YOU NOTICE?

FRONT   BACK

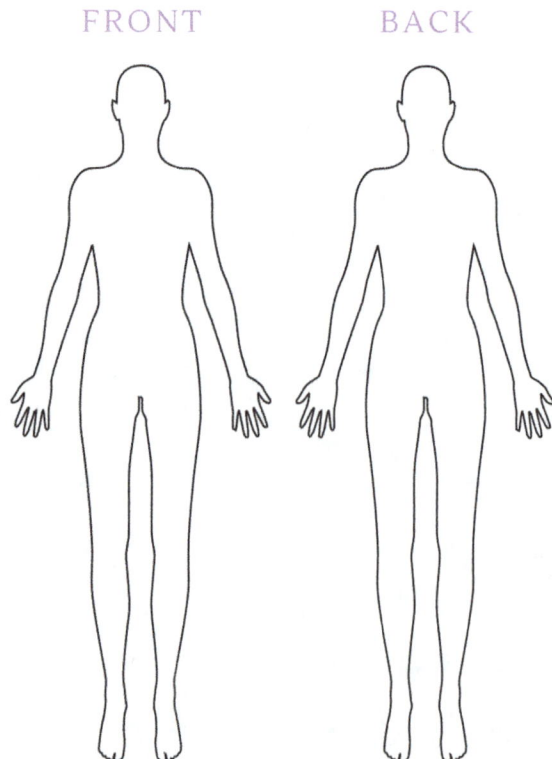

88

56. Contemplate the world's many illusions and dissolve into true seeing.

Most people's senses have such a limited ability to perceive the world. This practice invites you to deeply understand that humans cannot see all light, cannot hear all sound, or comprehend all ideas. This means that our understanding of the world is an incomplete picture, an illusion.

There is still so much that science does not understand about the nature of reality. This meditation opens the door to that mystery and suggests a contemplation of the stories that you write about world. It suggests you see past those stories to a deeper truth.

See past the surface of your experience all the way down to the tiniest quantum level where all that exists, all that we know, is just an ocean of waving particles of energy. Everything that we touch is energy held so tightly that we call it matter. At this level, there are no jobs, no borders, no countries, no social status, no religion. The world you experience is simply due to your senses and size. It is only limited by your narrative.

WHAT DO YOU NOTICE?

FRONT   BACK

57. In response to a strong desire, be still.
Observe the wave as it passes through you.

The times when you have an overwhelming urge to do something are the times when it is most important to stop and reflect. As desire asks you to act, instead sit still and ask the desire to move through you. Where in your body do you feel it the most?

You may find that desire will not be still, rather the longer you sit in inaction with it, the more it transforms within you. Notice the yearning shifts shapes and moves as you meet it with breath, intention, and visualization.

As temptation builds in you like churning water, let your breath create an ever expanding container that has room for every wave. Allow each exhale to soothe the waters of your desire, absorbing its energy and filtering out the deeper truth and lessons it contains. Realize that no desire is too big for you to sit with, no wave of urgency lasts forever. Breathe, let it pass, and you will see the sacred truth it leaves behind.

WHAT DO YOU NOTICE?

FRONT   BACK

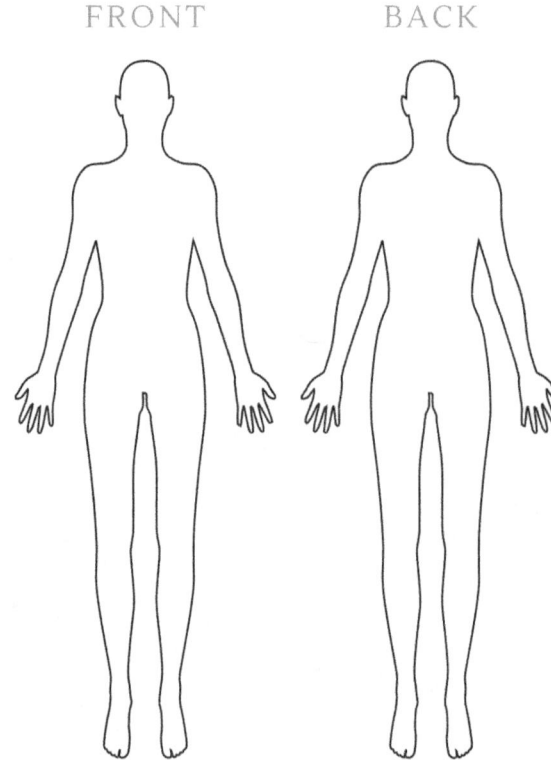

58.

Remember the world is simply a collection of stories. Find the truth in seeing yourself as both character and author.

The human brain is nothing short of a miraculous supercomputer. It engages in a near constant process of taking sensory input and weaving it into a cohesive narrative of a personal reality. It digests past experiences in an attempt to glean what might come next.

The issue here is that, due to the vast limitations of your senses, the stories that your brain creates are woefully incomplete, if not outright false. This understanding is a core pillar of the tantric worldview. These narrative stories from the brain are called Vikalpas and you are empowered to step into your role as the author of your journey.

As you write your mental stories, be mindful to ground them with compassion into a greater spiritual context. Write your stories as an optimistic realist. Tell your narrative in a voice that embraces the paradoxical truths of the world with grace, courage, and curiosity. Remember that you are ever evolving and so is everything and everyone else. In the end step out of the story all together and just exist.

WHAT DO YOU NOTICE?

FRONT   BACK

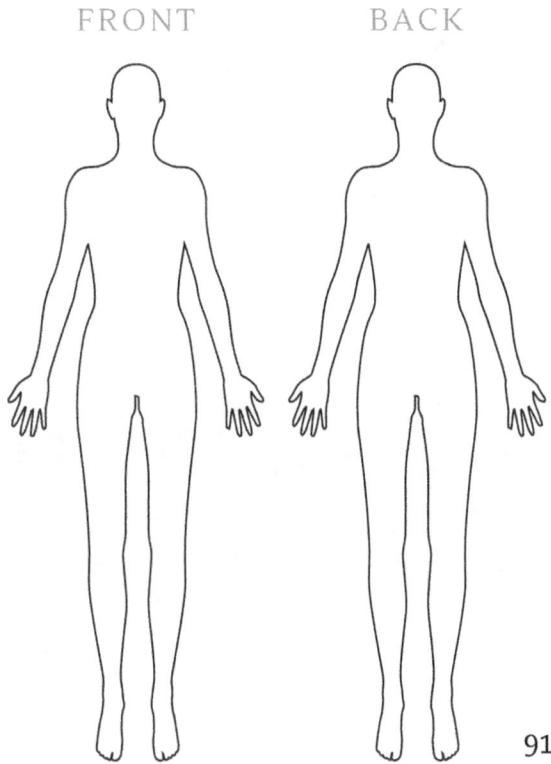

91

59. When faced with either/or try choosing both/and. Intentionally coexist with paradox.

The nature of the illusory world is to present situations in which you feel you must choose between two contradictory ways of acting or thinking. However, the more you apply this practice, the more you will see how the answer often lies in accepting and navigating multiple truths.

For a common example, when told to calm down, the quick reaction from most people is to say. "I am calm!" This is because some part of you is always a calm observer of the world. At the same time, you may be expressing or feeling the opposite of calm. Both are true. Consider this- not only are you upset, a part of you is also calm. It is almost always best to let the calm lead, even when moving with compassionate severity.

Coexisting with paradox is learning how to work with life's many polarities. Not only are you serious, you also play. Not only are you feminine, you are also masculine. Not only angry, also compassionate. As you embrace your many truths, you expand your capacity to embrace life itself.

WHAT DO YOU NOTICE?

FRONT   BACK

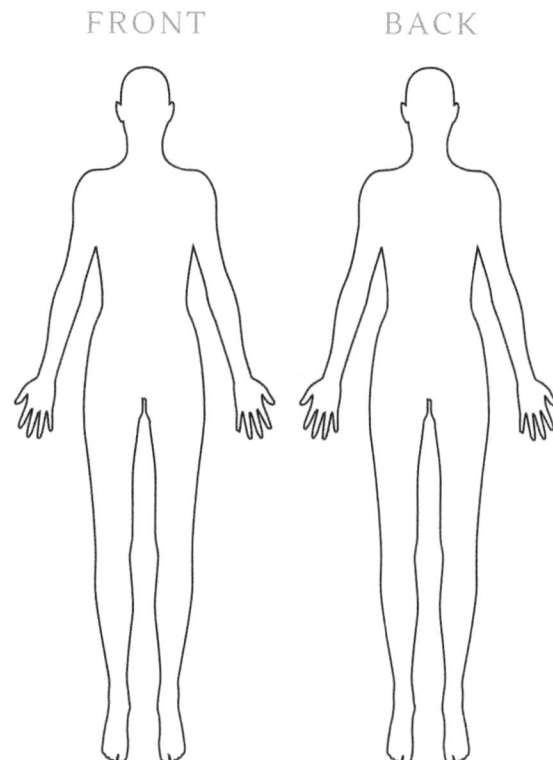

60.

Accept all things as expressions of divine consciousness in varying states of concealment.
In this acceptance find transformation.

All beings have the same spark of ever-present awareness that sits back and witnesses existence. In the tantric worldview, this conscious center is absolutely divine.

Each individual must forget its own divine nature in order to have a unique existence. If you were born and remembered that you are always connected to cosmic home, then perhaps you would never seek, you would never feel the need to create or grow. Challenging life experiences can drape over like lampshades and dim the light of sacred clarity, of clean perception.

This practice asks you to understand that even the most hateful people, the creepiest bugs, and the most aggressive animals have the same spark of conscious awareness. Each being is trying to make sense of existence, to survive and thrive. The illusion of disconnection creates harshness and this practice does not excuse that. Instead it asks for the most divine approach- find compassion for all. Show shadow what it means to be light.

WHAT DO YOU NOTICE?

FRONT   BACK

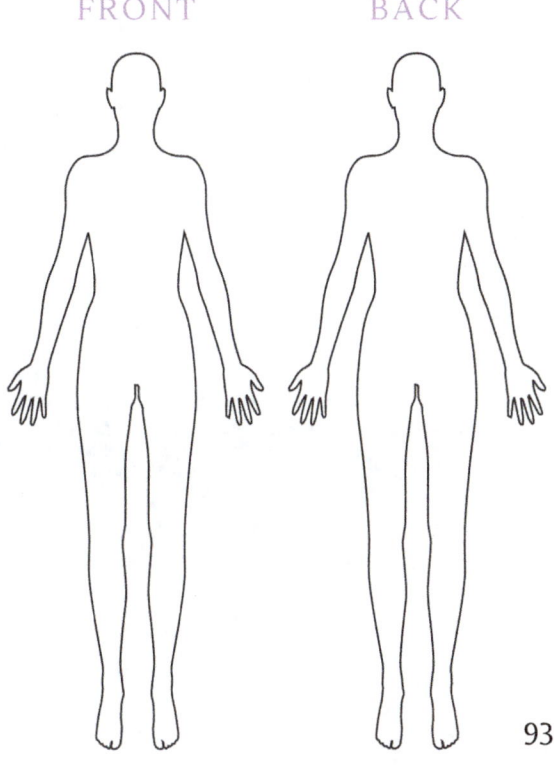

93

61. Contemplate all reality as waves, an emanation, rising and falling from the ocean of consciousness.

Modern physics has long understood that on the smallest scales the universe is made up of unfathomably tiny parts that exist as both particles and waves, depending on when or how they are observed. Moreover, researchers have recently seen that even the very fabric of time and space is rocked by vast waves. Like an ocean, the whole universe is waving, both on the largest and smallest levels.

The tantric worldview suggests that consciousness itself is the ground beneath time and space in its omnipresence and waving nature. Thoughts rise and fall in your mind, words rise and fall from your mouth, and you rise and fall from sleep. Your very existence rises up from the ocean of universal, ever-glowing consciousness before eventually falling back into oneness.

See this ebbing and flowing nature all around and in all things. See how all existence not only rides the wave, but also emerges from its waters.

WHAT DO YOU NOTICE?

FRONT   BACK

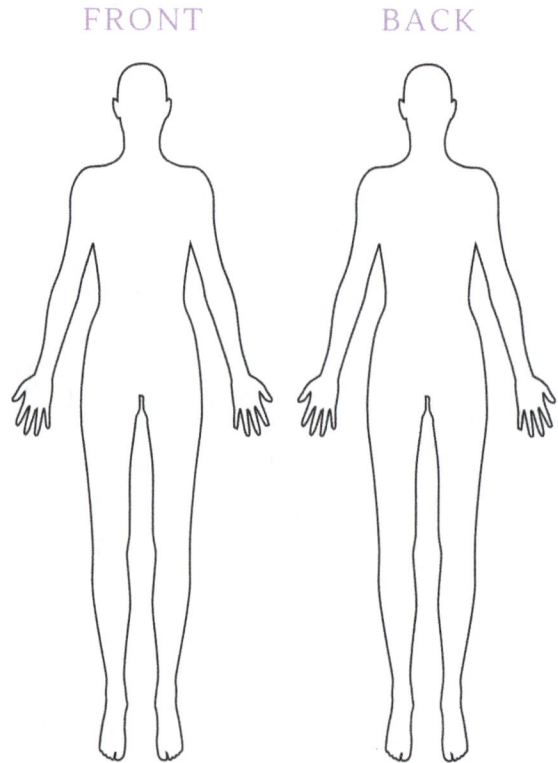

94

62.

Watch as though each thought is a painting.
Let the museum of your mind become the meditation.
Bliss is here too.

Many understand meditation as a practice of completely clearing the mind of all thoughts. For a few practices that is indeed the goal, but not all. Meditation can truly be anything that you engage in with full presence, breath, and visualization. Even exploring the busy museum of your mind can open you to a peaceful respite.

This technique asks you to turn your gentle awareness to the gallery of thoughts and stories created by your brain. As though soaking in an intricate painting, deeply observe one thought from a detached and curious perspective. Consider the root of this thought, where it began or what sparked it. Notice what this thought grows into and how it shifts under the gaze of your attention. Seek to compassionately understand it before moving onto the next.

When you step back from this technique, see a diverse collection of art that is your story of this life. Linger in the miracle of your mind's creations.

WHAT DO YOU NOTICE?

FRONT   BACK

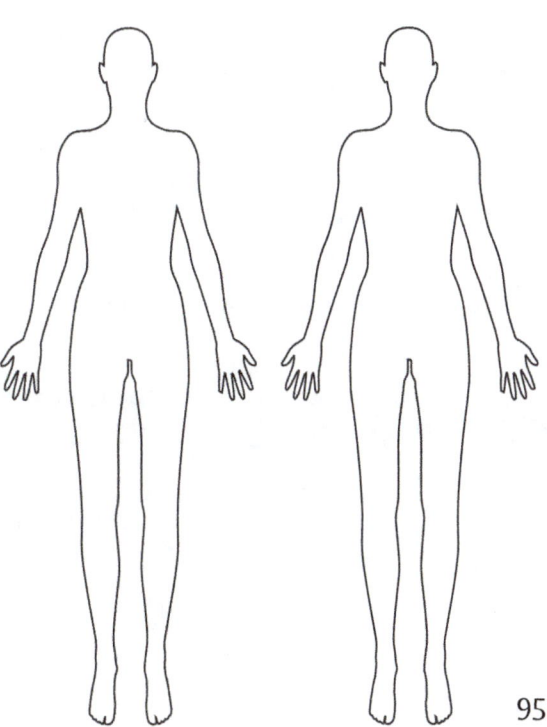

63. When a particular sense is heightened, let it become your whole being.

Upon smelling a delicious meal, gazing at a piece of enthralling art, dipping yourself in a hot bath, or hearing your favorite song- linger in the sensation. Stay with the particular sense that has overtaken you. Fully surrender to the experience until it is all you feel.

These moments can often be fleeting. Pure sensory joy is lost when interrupted by a thought or a distraction. When eating you think of work, when being touched you worry of the other person's thoughts, when smelling smoke you think of the flame. This practice opens the door for you to come present to sensation and awaken to its many subtleties.

This is a celebration of one single sense in a given moment. Whichever it is, encourage your whole being to feel it. Melt totally into a fully conscious experience of this one sensory stimulus. Become the bath, become the meal, become the song, and find yourself becoming aware of something new.

WHAT DO YOU NOTICE?

FRONT   BACK

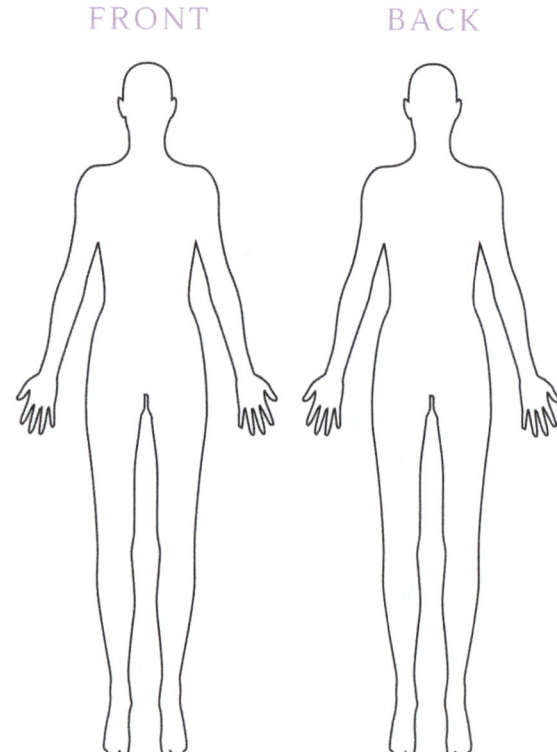

64. At the moment an intense feeling or experience arises in your body, awaken.

When caught up in the mind and the mundane events of the day it is natural to fall out of touch with your body. When it sends a signal, like an itch or an emotion, the natural response is to react immediately. Scratch the itch right away. If anxiety arises, fidget. If anger arises, perhaps your words lash out without a thought.

Try this- when a strong feeling arises in you, breathe deeply, turn your awareness towards it, and awaken to the nuances of that experience. Observe the sensation or emotion closely and use your breath to regulate the energy moving around your body. Only then, respond.

This exercise is a gateway to becoming more present to and conscious of your feelings- whatever they may be. If you can sit, even briefly, with a sensation then it will not control you. Of course this is easier said than done. The strongest feelings prompt the strongest urge to act. That is why this practice has the potential to be so awakening.

WHAT DO YOU NOTICE?

FRONT   BACK

65. Withhold judgment of anything as good or bad, spiritual or earthly. Therein expand your experience.

Wise teachers across a variety of spiritual lineages often tell their students that the single most divine skill to cultivate is compassion. When powerful gentleness is applied to any given situation, there is immense potential for sacred evolution and connection.

As a practice, this meditation invites you to find understanding and context for all things. Remember that each conscious being houses a divine light in their core. Even the most evil people have this light that has been muddied and shaded by a lifetime, or even generations, of hardship and perceived separation from others. This is not about creating excuses, it's about being able to hold paradox. It is about finding understanding for other people's values, tastes, beliefs, or even actions.

It is so easy to pass judgment on others based on the truths that you think you know of the world. While it is important to use discernment in choosing your own path, it is not for you to judge the path of another. In compassion find truth.

WHAT DO YOU NOTICE?

FRONT   BACK

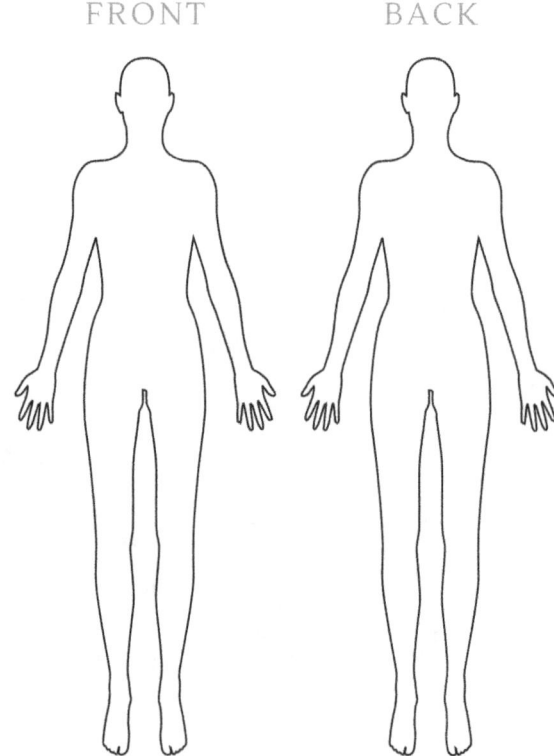

98

66.

Unfold the impermanent layers of your self to find the seed in you that will never change. Now do the same for others.

A central teaching in the tantric worldview is to be distinctly mindful of how you identify yourself and your sense of well being. It teaches that you will find misery if you attach your identity and contentment to a career, a person, a state of mind, or a way of looking. Your physical body will deteriorate, you car will wear down, your career will end over time, and your favorite shirt will eventually have holes.

Consider the many layers of yourself and how they change. Your material things, your body, your cravings, your emotions/thoughts, and even the void of your meditative state. All these things are impermanent. Unfold each of these realities and discover the piece of you that has stayed consistent through it all.

Uncover your center, your observer, your very own spark of everglowing consciousness. As the world shifts, as time wears on, know that each person carries such a seed within.

WHAT DO YOU NOTICE?

FRONT   BACK

67. Surrender to impermanence.
Contemplate change as the only constant.

This too shall pass. Nothing lasts forever. Even the plastics in our ocean will dissolve and disappear in a couple million years, a mere blink of an eye to the cosmos. Who knows where humans will be by then? The things in life that you adore and the things in life that you detest- all of it will change and take new form eventually.

Consider how much suffering you can shed when you allow yourself to accept the simple fact that change is constant. You can accept the existence of loathsome things, knowing there is at least some small aspect that you can change to make it better. You can stop suffering from the anxiety of losing what you love, knowing that, yes, it will be lost.

Surrender to this reality and commit to making the most of each living moment with those you love and doing the things that you most cherish. Surrender to the eternal truth of change as the only constant in life. Melt into pure presence to make the most of each ever-changing moment.

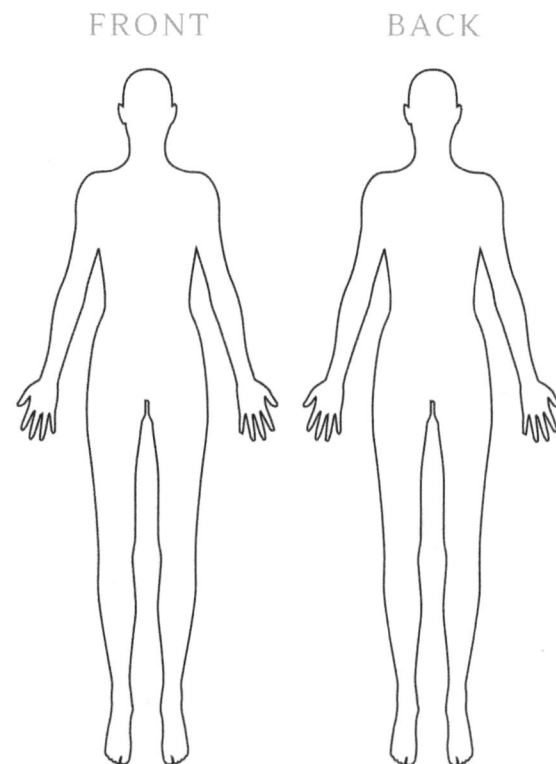

WHAT DO YOU NOTICE?

FRONT   BACK

68.

Don't wait for your dreams. Take action each day, however small. Go beyond hoping to experience true living.

You may feel overwhelmed by the thought of achieving your dreams. Perhaps your heart's visions are so big, so inspired, that when you zoom back into the present moment, all the steps to make it a reality feel unachievable.

However, even the biggest dreams are possible in some form. This exercise asks you to take a dream that you have been carrying and go a step beyond hoping that it will come true. If you dream of being an opera singer, start practicing vocal exercises each day. If you dream of studying the stars, start with a book and an outside chair on a starry night.

The world is a balance of fate and free will, the individual and the community. Take your will, your individual energy, and direct it towards a dream, even in the smallest way. Keep doing this, keep showing up, day after day. If you do this, fate and community will come meet you in the middle. Fully engage in manifestation with this practice.

WHAT DO YOU NOTICE?

FRONT   BACK

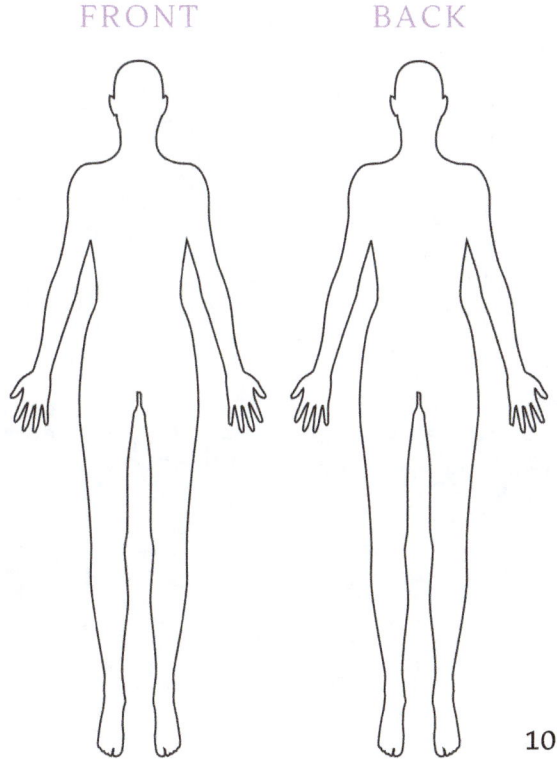

69.

Understand the thing you rebel against controls you.
Choose the heart's genuine path
and find real freedom.

A natural result of being born a human is an individuation from universal consciousness, a deep forgetting of your vast, conscious, omniscient, and omnipresent existence.

Born into a body, you slowly relearn existence from those who raise you. You learn a world full of black and white thinking, full of rules, many of which you may not understand or accept. In such a world, the pendulum can swing drastically from one extreme to another. When told no, you say, "Yes!" simply to assert yourself. But that is the crux of this practice.

When you make a choice as a reaction, is it really your choice or were you pushed into it from a place of resistance? Understand that which you push against will push back with equal force. Contemplate the direction you truly want to go. Listen closely to your whole body- head, heart, and gut. Discover what is really in your highest interest and find real freedom to be your true self.

WHAT DO YOU NOTICE?

FRONT   BACK

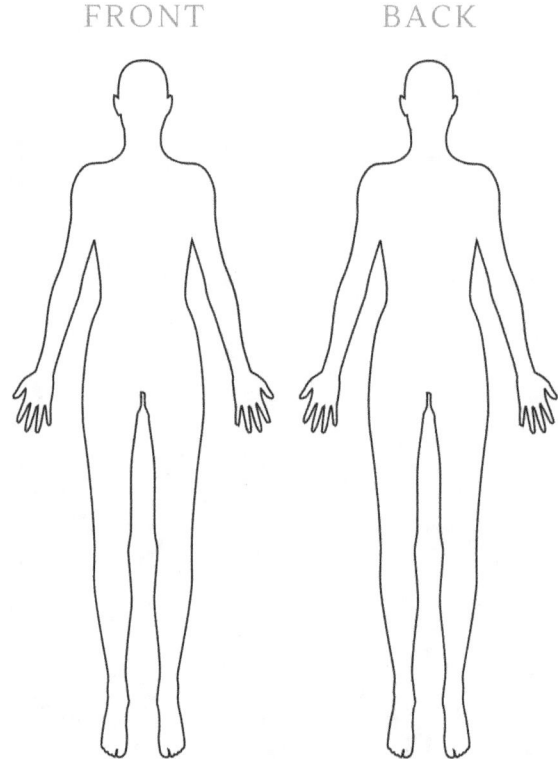

70. Envision a bright, clear light moving up your spine as you breathe.

Constantly shifting experiences of daily life can leave you feeling ungrounded, disjointed, or totally disconnected from your innate spiritual power. Tantra teaches of a central channel of energy that runs the length of the spine and can support you in healing this disconnection. The channel, Sushumna, reconnects you to heaven and earth, to divine masculine and divine feminine, and to pure consciousness and pure energy.

Invite your awareness to drop into your root chakra at the base of your spine. Taking a deep breath, let your focus visualize a bright shaft of light. With your next breath, feel this light begin to grow up and around your spine. Take your time, deepen your breath even more. Stay connected to this imagery of light rising and glowing within you.

Notice your body extend as the beam reaches your head. Exhale deeply and see it blossom from your crown, unfolding its petals to the sky, and connecting you both above and below.

WHAT DO YOU NOTICE?

FRONT   BACK

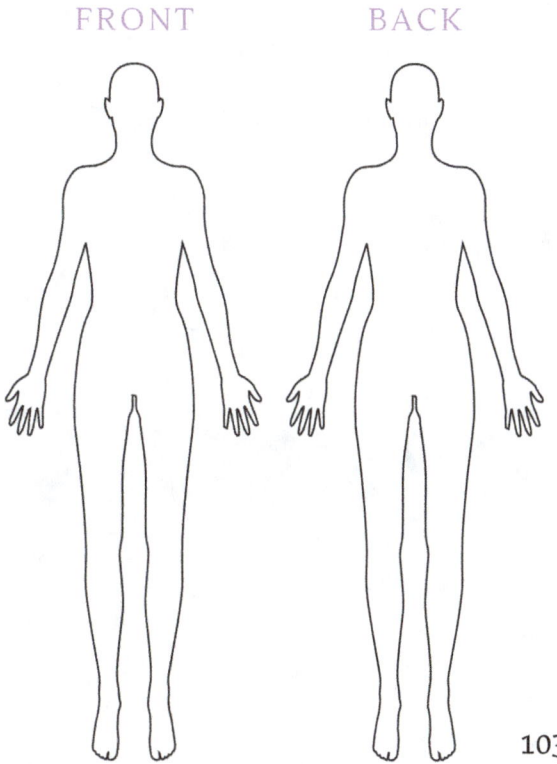

71. Vividly imagine a warm light bouncing between your chakras.

As though lightning itself could be gentle, allow it to enter into the crown of your head with a deep inhale, igniting a spark of pure consciousness. With your next breath feel that spark bounce down to awaken your third eye, the intuitive center between your brows. Breathe again as warm light jumps into your throat chakra, the realm of hearing and speaking truth.

Notice the light ricochet around and land in the center of your heart chakra, illuminating pure love, compassion, and forgiveness. It then skips down into your solar plexus and awakens a sense of courage and personal power. With another exhale, the light moves down to your sacral chakra, home to your sexuality, passion, and creativity.

Lastly, let your breath and the warm light ease into your perineum, the root chakra. Feel it connect you to a sense of purpose and belonging on this planet. Now notice what seeds grow within you when you try this exercise in reverse.

WHAT DO YOU NOTICE?

FRONT   BACK

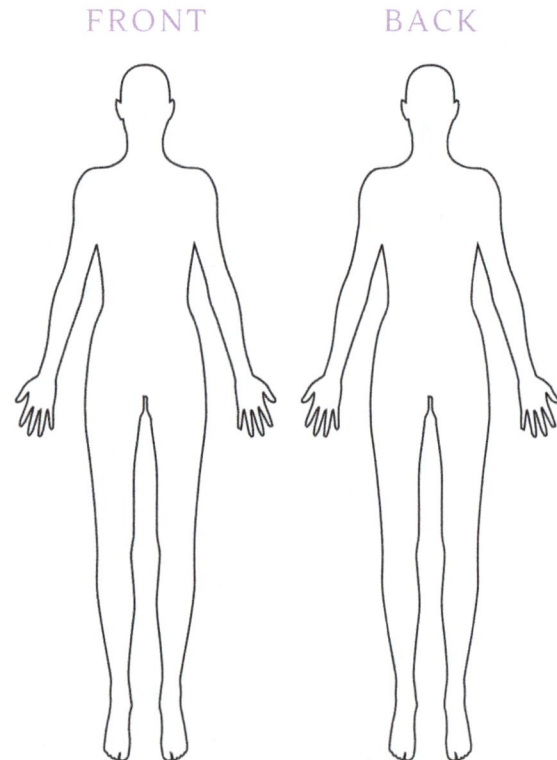

72. Contemplate the whole universe as alive and immortal.

What does it really mean for something to be alive? Is it true that, "I think, therefore I am."? Does this mean that plants think, that a jellyfish thinks, even without a brain? We know they are alive. Researchers watch plants and even molds appear to respond to the world and make decisions accordingly. This surely implies some basic form of consciousness.

Tantric teachings suggest that consciousness itself is a fundamental underpinning of the universe, much like how we perceive time and space, only even more primordial. It is the fabric or the container for all that exists. It posits that on some level, the act of observing is inherent in all things. That even a stone is having a very slow, very muted experience of what it is to be a stone.

What does this mean on a cosmic scale? Ponder the nature of a universe that is always observing and being observed. If awareness is universal, can it ever really die? Imagine the infinite wisdom contained in the immortal awareness of ever-present consciousness.

WHAT DO YOU NOTICE?

FRONT   BACK

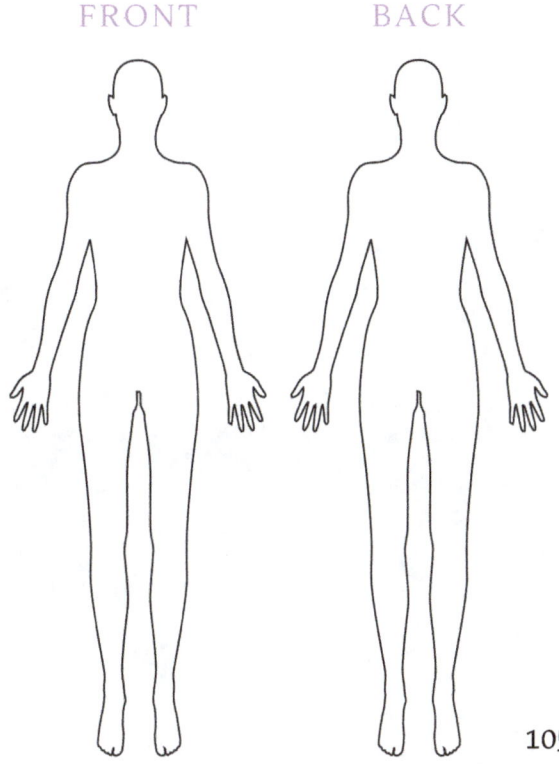

73. Let your consciousness dissolve into the cerulean blue of a clear sky.

Remember a time when you found yourself outside, gazing out into a clear blue sky, casually observing the abyss that is concealed behind it. This is something that is human nature to do, however it is most often practiced without intention.

This time, go outside on a clear, sunny day and try this with conscious curiosity. Notice not one shade of blue, but many tones seamlessly blended together above your head. As you gaze straight up into the deepest cerulean blue, become aware of something beyond. Notice a luminous glow within this blue.

Awaken to the same luminous void within yourself. Stare into the clear blue sky and then close your eyes, capturing the same clarity within. Let this exercise guide you in clearing the fog of your own mind and body. Allow your awareness and your whole being to dissolve into crisp, blue, endless firmament.

WHAT DO YOU NOTICE?

FRONT   BACK

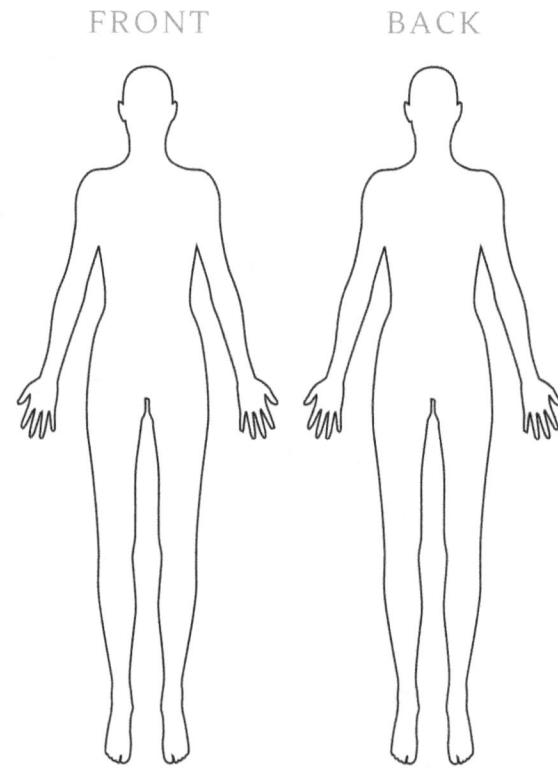

74.

As above, so below. As outside, so inside.
Understand the whole cosmos
to exist in your head.

Tantric philosophy spends a lot of time exploring the concepts of duality and polarity. In teaching its practitioners to transcend the confines of dualistic thinking, it does not turn away from or deny duality itself. Instead polarity becomes a tool for expanding your ability to move through life with wisdom and contentment.

Tantra invites you to explore both sides of polarity so that you can contain all truths and nestle peacefully in the center. It suggests that everything you see in the world is also reflected within you. Not only beauty, but pain. Not only sorrow, but wisdom as well.

Indeed, your vast inner world is a microcosm of the whole universe. The same infinite potential for creation, evolution, maintenance, death, and rebirth is alive in both you and the cosmos. Allow this reality to sink in, to fuse into you. Like the cosmos, you have the power to create your own world, it's all within you.

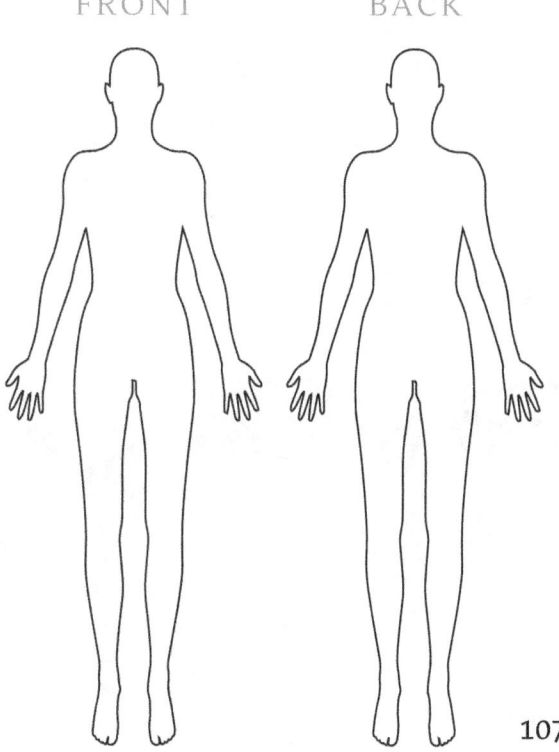

WHAT DO YOU NOTICE?

FRONT   BACK

75.
Remember you are made of light.
Let that remembrance change you.

Gaze softly at a fire or a gentle light, allowing its radiance to warm your eyes and whole being. With fascination, notice the character and movement of this glowing, mysterious aspect of reality. Let your consciousness merge with luminescence.

The quality of conscious awareness itself is light in another form. Whatever you turn your focus towards is spotlighted and revealed from the shadows, whether it is a messy basement or a long hidden emotion. When a fact comes to light, it is because our witnessing illuminates it.

This contemplative exercise invites you to turn this light inward to see that your whole body is alive with awareness. The miracle of your nervous system allows you to awaken every corner of your being. Awaken your toes, your spine, your belly, and your heart. Feel the lights turn on within, feel yourself ignite your own ever-glowing truth. In this practice, see that you are not only filled with light, but that it is your very nature.

WHAT DO YOU NOTICE?

FRONT   BACK

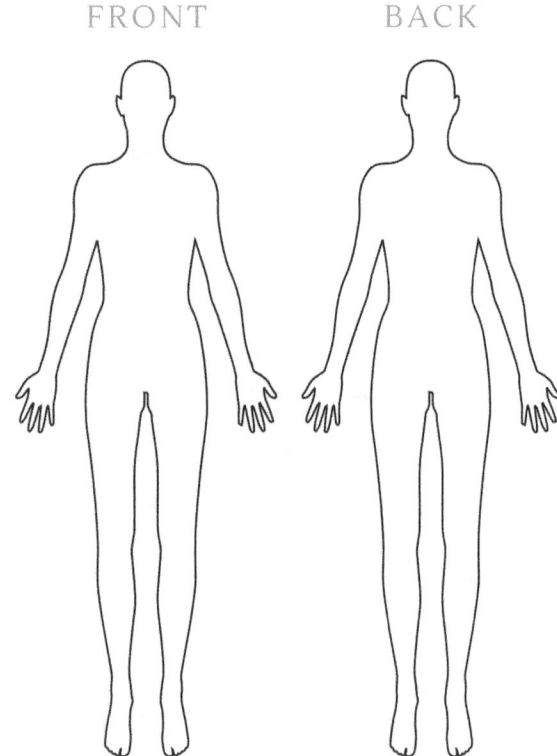

76. Become one with a completely dark room, a cave, a moonless night.

Most people have experienced the feeling of being afraid in the dark. It is a natural response to instead create a light to feel safe amongst the shadows. But this exercise explores the other end of that spectrum. Imagine that you are nocturnal, that the cover of darkness becomes your place of safety. Visualize trusting the embrace of darkness when the lights go off or when the moon is hidden.

Notice each of your senses shift and adjust to the lightless environment. How does the rest of your body engage to compensate for the lack of sight? How do your eyes themselves respond when there is no input? Become aware of the edges of your being when you are unable to distinguish them from the space around you.

Explore the void of form and formlessness from a new perspective. Deeply experience blackness until you come upon the ever-glowing truth that is there in the dark with you, and in you.

WHAT DO YOU NOTICE?

FRONT   BACK

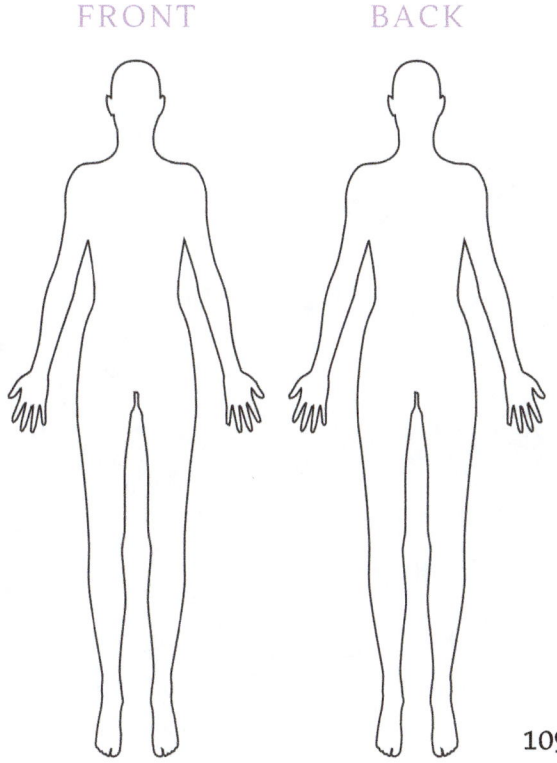

People spend so much of their waking life immersed in the story of their daily existence. For those with an inner dialogue, there is a constant narration of past, present, and future experiences. Even those without narration are in a state of constantly responding and reacting to their experienced reality, the plot of their life.

Close your eyes, breathe deeply, and pause the story. Let the curtains fall across the stage of your life, let the spotlights drop, and rest quietly in your own darkness. In darkness there is stillness and in stillness there is peace. Feel your way around the darkened room of your insides and find that it contains a whole universe of potential.

Notice how expansive that inner universe is and how its darkness softly invites you to come rest. Contrary to fearsome darkness, this blackness within embraces you in a loving, rejuvenating shadow each night. A closed-eye respite that is there even in the day, even in the light we so love.

WHAT DO YOU NOTICE?

FRONT BACK

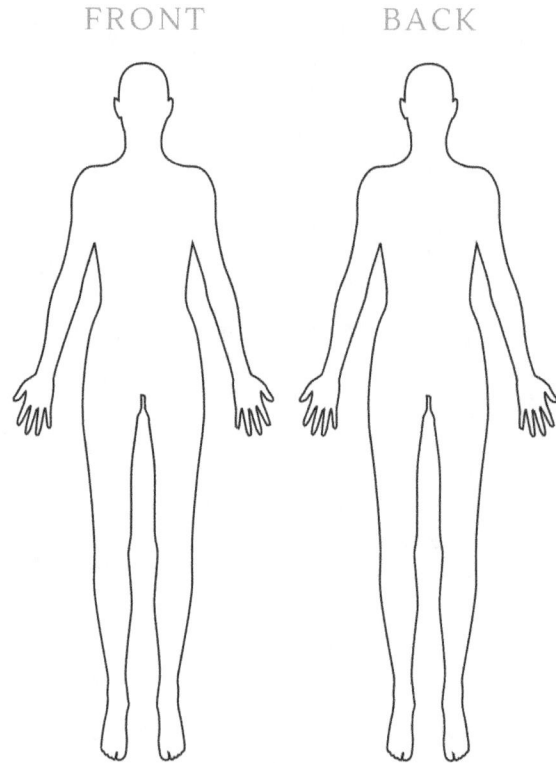

78. When something has caught your full attention, notice. Cultivate true presence.

Cultivating deep presence takes practice. Attention is always on the move, jumping from one thing to another, focusing and refocusing in an often disjointed way. Buddha called this the monkey mind, as though your mind is akin to a monkey inside the house of your body. The monkey runs from room to room, looking out every window and opening every door. Meditation is akin to bringing the monkey something shiny to coax it into sitting still.

This technique invites you to take advantage of a moment when your mind has found something shiny. It asks you to linger on whatever has caught your focus, to stretch out your attention, and to cultivate your ability to remain present.

Maybe it is a campfire under the stars, maybe it is a song, maybe it is the eyes of a lover, or the waves on a beach. When it has completely captured your attention, awaken to the moment, exist only in the present.

WHAT DO YOU NOTICE?

FRONT   BACK

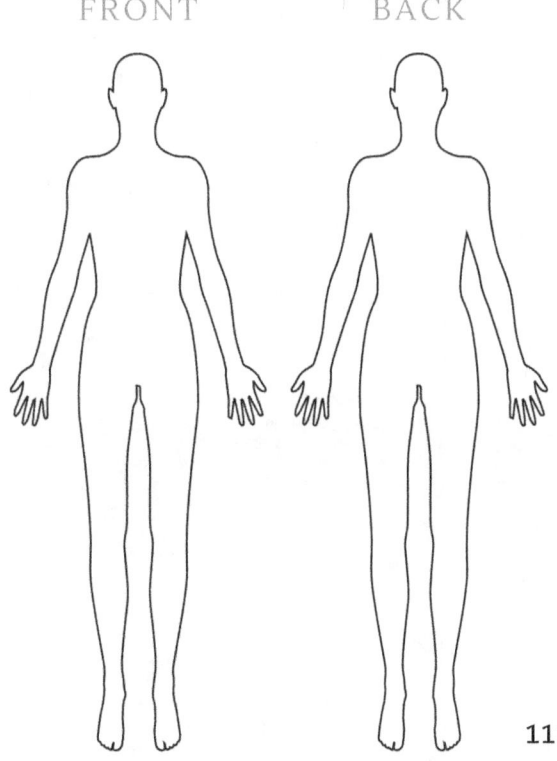

79.

**Envision a fire burning within your body,
transforming all to ashes,
leaving only your center untouched.**

Consider trying this on a cold day. Close your eyes and imagine that your belly is built up into a fireplace. As you breathe, a flame starts small and begins to grow, radiating heat up and down your spine. Feel the flames growing increasingly hot as the warmth expands to fill your extremities.

As you continue to breathe and focus on the visual of the fire, imagine dropping a pain from your heart down into the blaze and watching as it burn to ashes. Let this growing inferno burn all things within you that challenge you, let them be taken away and transformed into something new. Now do the same with all that you love about yourself and your story. Simply let it go.

Allow all of you, this whole lifetime of joy and pain, physical and mental, to burn into a pile of ashes. Take close notice of the part of you that watches and does not burn. Let that center linger in the pile of ashes that was you. Continue to watch as a wisdom, unique to your life, sprouts up from the rubble.

WHAT DO YOU NOTICE?

FRONT   BACK

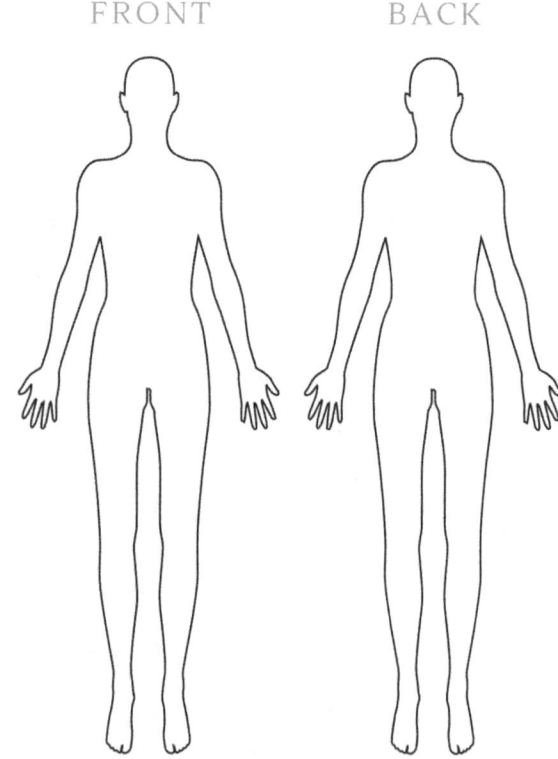

80.

Transcend the human experience by envisioning the whole illusory world burning to ashes. Then what?

This practice has been a real life experience to countless humans who have lost everything in a blaze. Step back from the personal stories around it and see the true nature of fire as an ancient force on our planet. For eons fire has shaped and decimated landscapes, scorching everything in its path. The flames are indifferent. Both destructive and constructive, the ashes it leaves behind create the fertile land that life needs to rebuild.

This technique asks you to deeply ponder this aspect of reality. It asks you to envision the whole world we humans have created just burning to the ground. All the buildings, all the trash, all computers and books- everything.

Why? To remind you of the impermanence of our stories and belongings. It is to remind you to both detach from them and appreciate them in a whole new way. This practice reminds you what is possible, even when you think that all is lost.

WHAT DO YOU NOTICE?

FRONT   BACK

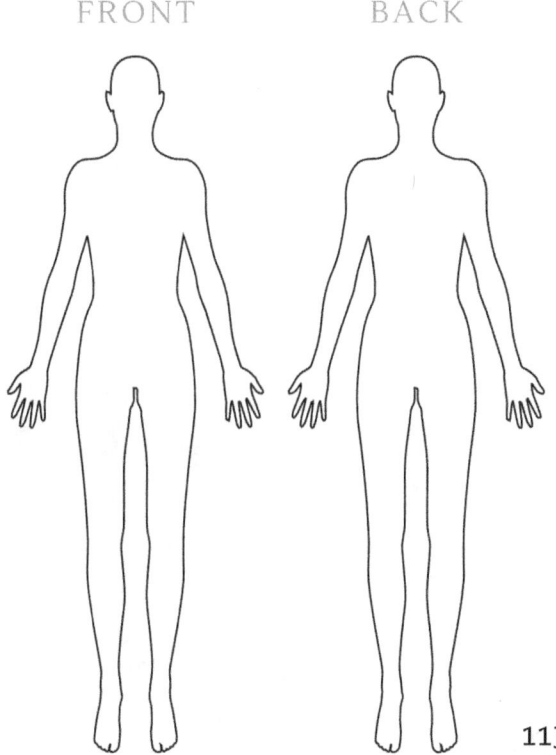

81. With total surrender, find that all things converge in your divine self.

To consider all things converging in you, both beautiful and repugnant, may feel intimidating or even like a bad idea. However, this practice asks you not to turn away from the world and not to reject any part of it as separate from the divine.

Tantra is often understood as teachings that weave the world together. It interlaces the spiritual and the material, the masculine and the feminine, the inner world and the outer world. It weaves light and shadow, beauty and pain, earth and heaven, all with the intention to empower the practitioner to learn the true compassionate nature of reality and their role in it.

This practice opens you to understanding that you are a part of this great tapestry, that it exists within you and all around you. When you surrender and remain open to all truths of the world, you awaken your divine ability to discern a path forward. You can connect with your sovereign position, intertwined with all threads.

WHAT DO YOU NOTICE?

FRONT   BACK

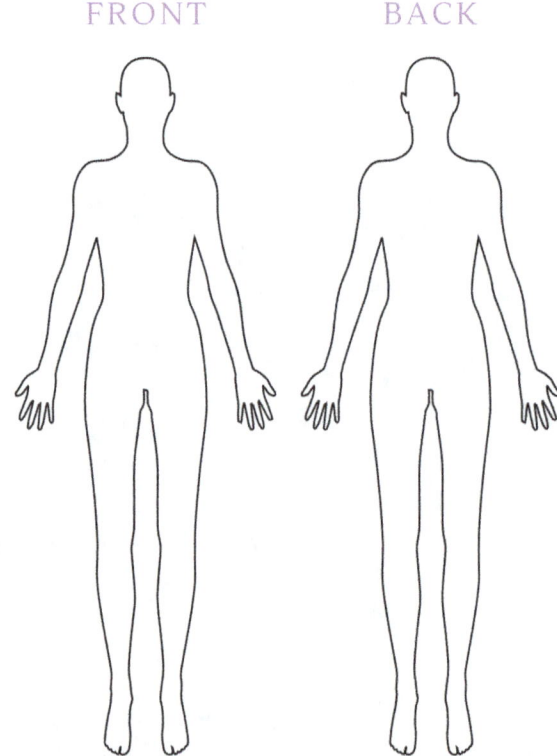

82. Experience without labeling, analyzing, or thinking at all.

A common theme across tantric ideology is the understanding that a typical human's perception of the world is dramatically limited. Senses can only perceive so much information, which leaves the brain and its interpretive abilities to make sense of the world.

Because of the way the mind filters information, the moment you begin to narrate or to analyze an experience, you stop seeing it for what it really is. Instead, the true reality of it gets warped into something more manageable to understand. To experience anything fully, you must put aside the brain's desire to describe it and just witness.

Give your attention fully to the senses that are experiencing a given thing. If you are watching musicians, take deep and singular notice of the sounds, the sights, and the vibrations in your body. If listening to a story, don't imagine where it will go next. If you have a vision, just be with it and wait until later to understand it. Simply observe.

WHAT DO YOU NOTICE?

FRONT   BACK

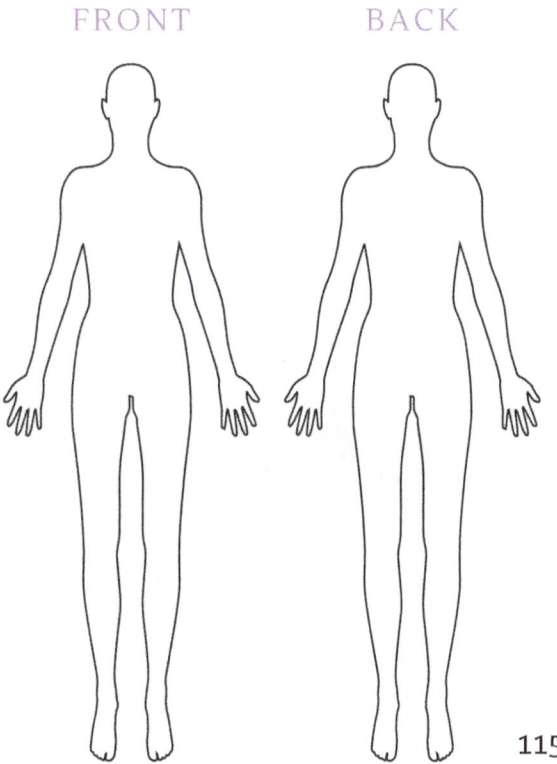

83.

Pause each time before saying "I am...".
Reflect on the miracle
that saying such a thing is even possible.

Do you ever wonder who you really are? What it means to be you? Stop and ponder this in a reflective way. "I am" is one of the most common ways to start a sentence. I am Hungry? Excited? Angry? Grateful? X years old? American? Short? Consider how many of these things will be true in five years, ten years, or even on the day you die.

Are you defined by your desires, your hunger, or your yearning? Consider whether your physical characteristics or nationality really define you. It is easy to identify and categorize yourself based on the qualities you think you know of the world and yourself.

Reflect on the quest you take in life to figure out who you are in the scheme of it all. Notice how many different versions of yourself have existed over time. Consider how many living beings coexist in this one body that gets to say, "I am." Through this practice, uncover all the transient layers and discover your true conscious self at the center of it all, the essence in the middle.

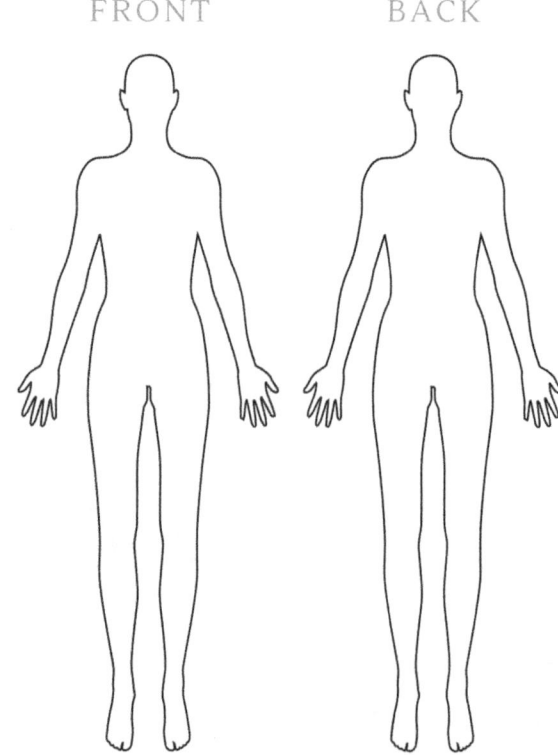

WHAT DO YOU NOTICE?

FRONT   BACK

84. Disidentify with your body. Joyously realize that your true being is so much bigger.

This is something that often happens to a person unintentionally. Someone may experience their consciousness leaving the body due to trauma, a near death experience, or a psychotropic substance. When inadvertently disidentifying with the body the results can be mixed. It can leave a person with a sense of wonder or feeling a deep confusion about their identity.

This exercise invites you to explore this experience with an intention to better know yourself and the nature of reality. Close your eyes, breathe deeply in through the nose, and connect with a visual of where consciousness is centered in your body. From this place, wherever it is within you, observe your body as though it belonged to someone else.

Bring that consciousness outside yourself and look in with curiosity, gentleness, and compassion. Notice how this expands your sense of self, revealing that you are not the vessel that contains you. Understand that you are far greater than this body you inhabit. You are both every thing and no thing.

WHAT DO YOU NOTICE?

FRONT   BACK

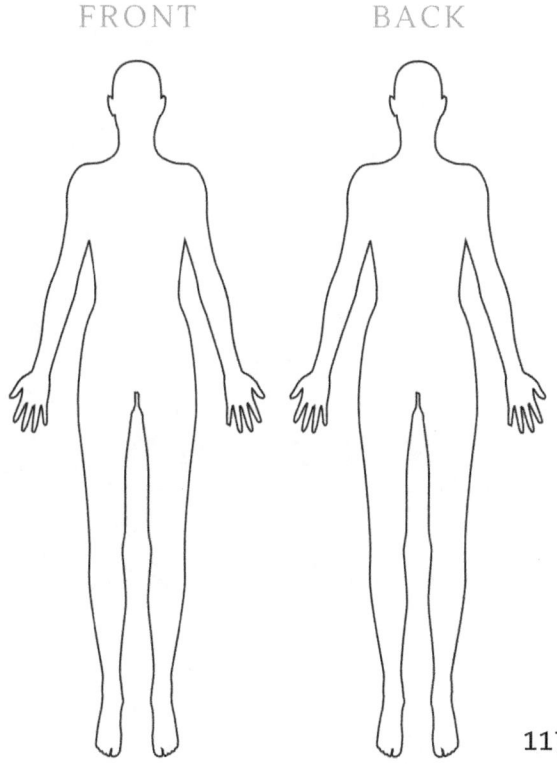

Meditate on no thing.
Let this expand you.

It is a common misconception that meditation is clearing the mind and thinking of nothing. In reality, to meditate on no thing is one of the more difficult practices in this collection.

Tantra posits that the whole universe is thought into existence when the field of divine consciousness dances with the divine field of pure energy. When the masculine meets the feminine. If something hasn't been thought of, then it doesn't exist. Before meeting energy, consciousness is just pure potential. Before meeting consciousness, energy can take no shape. Linger with that abstraction.

Consider the reality that existed before this dance of consciousness and energy. Let your mind stretch to perceive nothingness. As it wanders and ponders, keep coming back to no thing. What then? What do you discover? Are you, the observer, even observing if there is no subject? Consider whether there is even a distinction between your mind and no thing- for no thing has no boundaries, no edges, and no center. It is the soundless sound, the space beyond space.

WHAT DO YOU NOTICE?

FRONT   BACK

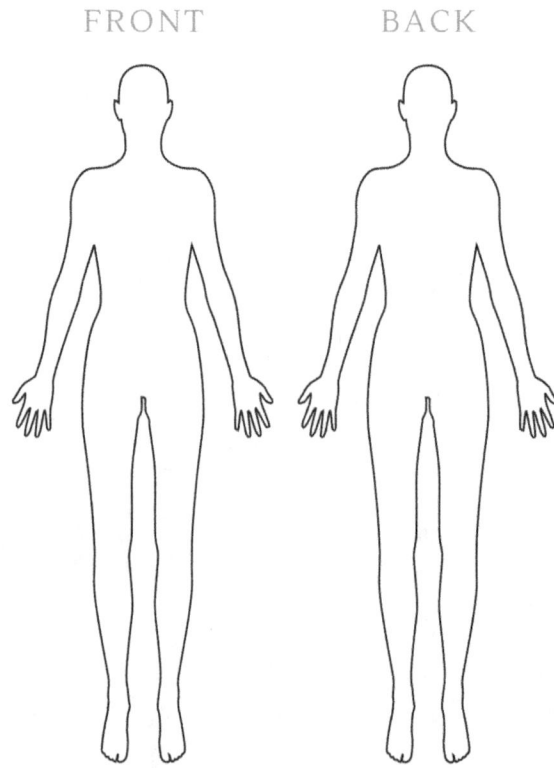

86.
Fathom the unfathomable.
Experience, beyond all we know.

Allow your mind to freely wander into its most mysterious curiosities and realms. Open to uncharted territories of thought and transcend the limitations of what you think to be possible.

Consider the beginning of time and what came before it. Consider the edges of the universe and what may lay beyond. Ponder a way of life that is vastly different than your own. Vividly create a creature in your mind that has never existed and then create a world for it to live in.

Let your mind stretch, warp, and open to a world in which anything is possible. Engage with and embrace the paradox of thinking the unthinkable. How can there be a time before time? How can atoms, molecules, and single cell organisms come together to create a body, much less a planet?

Fathom the unfathomable and discover that it is contained within you. Recognize that nothing is beyond your mind's reach.

WHAT DO YOU NOTICE?

FRONT   BACK

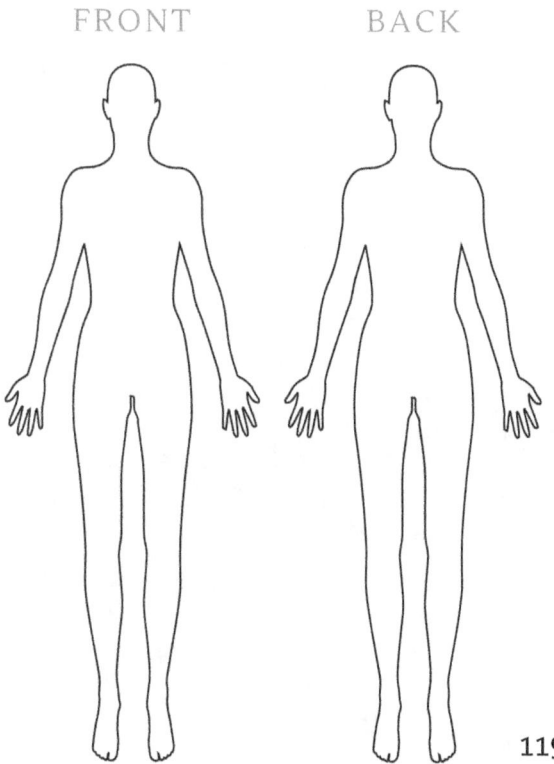

119

87.
Consider what it feels like to exist, to be.
In this reflection, see nothing that limits you.

Life requires so much maintenance. Consider all that you have to do to make your own life possible. You must eat, sleep, clean, manage, and most likely work to actively sustain it. This technique asks you to pause from all the doing and tap into what it means to simply exist.

Stop tasking and rest in stillness. What is your experience then? What does your existence feel like? Notice if you are tired, joyful, inspired, or anything else. Is the nature of existence in your senses or is it within your thoughts? Or is it somewhere else? As you contemplate, linger here in a state of pure being, pure experiencing.

In any present moment, start noticing that you can shift how it feels to exist. In sadness you can recreate your very existence to tune into a peaceful, accepting state of being. Through exploring this technique, learn that the nature of your existence is surprisingly malleable to your will. Find relief here.

WHAT DO YOU NOTICE?

FRONT   BACK

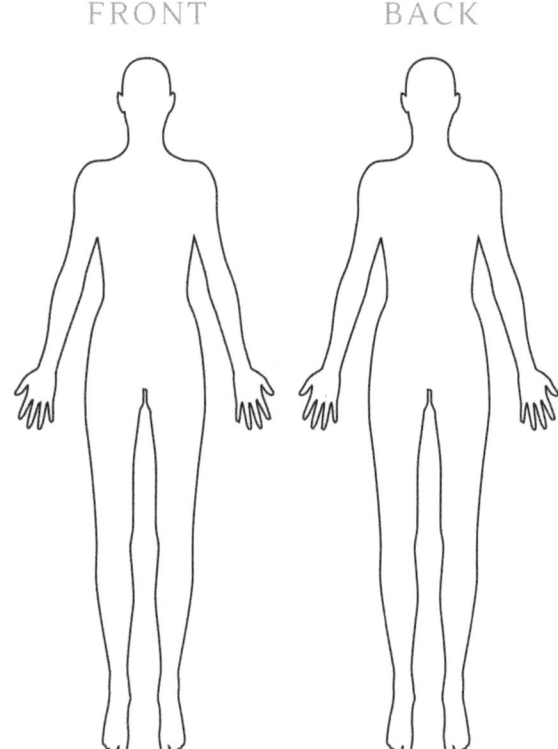

88.

Contemplate all existence as a relationship between observer, observed, and the act of observation- all expressions of consciousness.

In the tantric worldview, the entire cosmos consists of fields energy and consciousness that create what we know as matter and light. Each individual being represents a contraction or a condensation of consciousness and energy. From a universal, undifferentiated consciousness you become individuated from the whole, thus contracting your perspective and causing you to believe that your conscious self is separate from everything else. Many call this the illusion of separation.

Out from this individuated state comes you, the observer. Everything else is the observed and the act of observation is the tether connects you. All three of these distinct entities are in fact emanations from one ever-present consciousness that witnesses all. You are not separate from what you observe. "Enlightenment" is a shedding of this contracted sense of self. Not a destination, but a state of being that you may have even experienced before. Use this deeply esoteric practice to return home to this expansive state.

WHAT DO YOU NOTICE?

FRONT   BACK

121

89. Unify the many fragments of your inner experiences and sensations into one cohesive understanding.

This practice is an essential tool for anyone on the journey of healing and self knowledge. After a lifetime of both challenging and uplifting experiences, the memories, emotions, sensations, and lessons can be difficult to integrate.

You may deny emotions or memories that feel too heavy or conversely you may deny the parts of you that shine out of a fear of being seen. There may be whole regions of your inner world that feel beyond your comprehension. Despite all this, it is possible to expand your capacity to lovingly hold all of it.

This self study reflects on each fragment with acceptance, curiosity, and care. One by one, the puzzle pieces of your being come into clarity when illuminated by your gentle attention. As you give each piece a home within you, your propensity for self love grows, and the picture of you becomes increasingly clear, allowing a deeper sense of serenity and wisdom, both for yourself and others.

WHAT DO YOU NOTICE?

FRONT   BACK

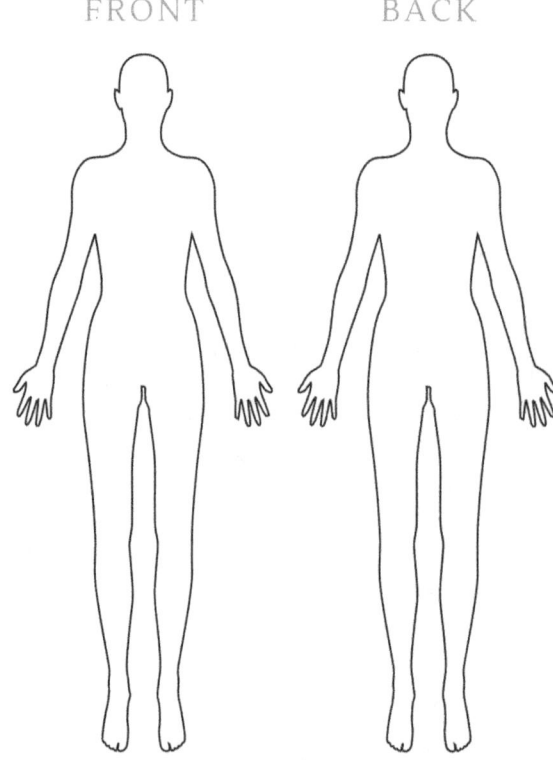

90.

Gently place the fingers over the eyes
until you also feel it in the heart.
When you feel it, find pain transmutes into peace.

Make yourself comfortable, place your fingers over your eyes, and breathe deeply. As your breath slows and deepens, bring your awareness to the sensations in your body. Visualize the many electric and magnetic currents running through you, from your nervous system to the blood in your veins. Take special notice of the charge running from your fingertips to your eyes.

Now, breathing, focusing, and visualizing, call that energy from your eyes, gently around your mind, and down into your heart. Quietly observe and breathe as your consciousness creates a warm glow that embraces all of you and activates this pathway with total acceptance and pure love.

Let yourself be creative with this visualization as it spreads through you. Maybe it feels like a warm glow, or a soft blanket, or even like cool water. This practice is a gateway to unite your consciousness to your energy, your mind to your heart, and your thoughts to your feelings. In this connection there is access to meaningful peace and stillness.

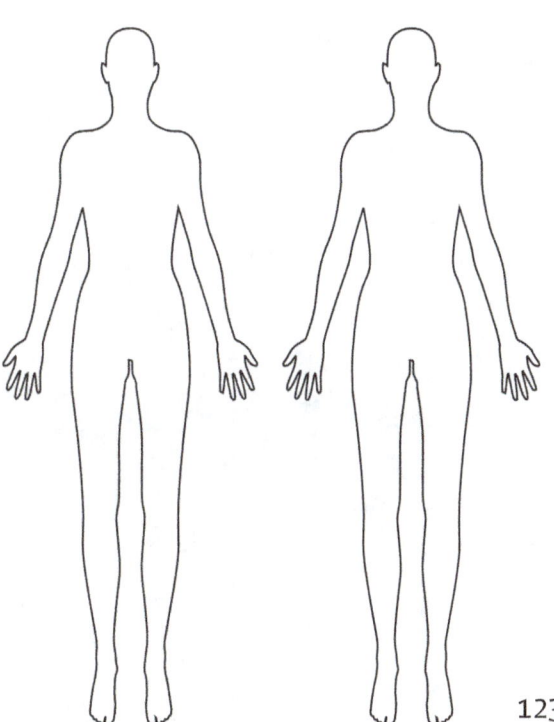

WHAT DO YOU NOTICE?

FRONT   BACK

123

91. Feel the unseen electromagnetism above you, below you, and emanating from you.

Take a deep dive into reality and contemplate the fact that every atom and molecule in your body, and in the whole universe, is held together by electromagnetism. Even the pumping of your heart creates a strong enough current to form a magnetic field. You are alive with electricity, your aura is a real bioelectric phenomenon around you.

Close your eyes, breathe deeply, and visualize this electricity in your body. Notice how it is affected by your breath, attention, and imagination. Linger here, feeling into your natural charge.

As you ponder this, take it one step further and remember that everything, from the floor underneath you to the air you breathe is sustained by the same electromagnetism that gives you form. Expand your focus and perceive how this subtle energy permeates seamlessly between yourself and the world around you. Let this expanded perception change and awaken you to the nature of this electric reality.

WHAT DO YOU NOTICE?

FRONT   BACK

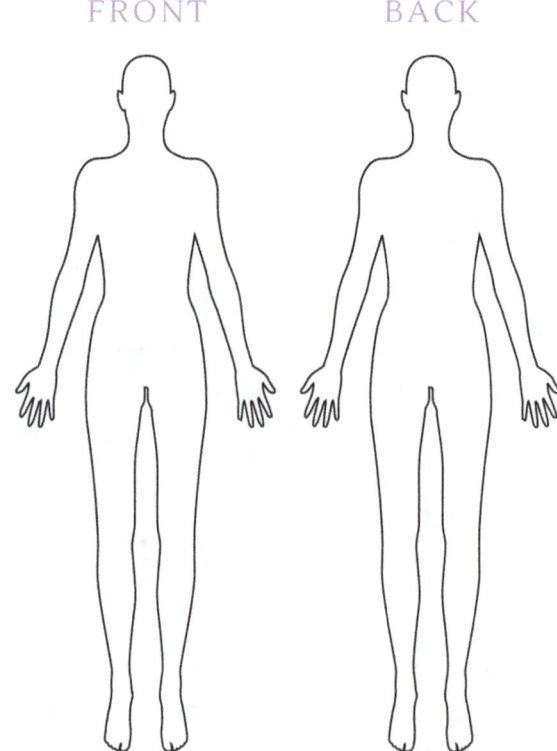

92. Notice when you are barely aware of your thoughts and feelings, when they are quiet enough to float delicately in your heart.

Even those with the busiest minds have moments when the stream of thoughts comes to a slow, quiet pause. Perhaps it is in a moment of awe, witnessing a beautiful landscape or dancing in a crowd at a concert. Perhaps it is on a bench in a crowded park when the sun shines down and clears the mind.

This technique prompts you to capture these moments when your thoughts are quiet or stop all together. Linger in the subtlety of the experience. Encourage your brain to simply observe instead of process.

Just watch, just feel, just breathe, and let the moment gently fill you. Give your mind an opportunity to absorb the expansive nature of reality that comes when thoughts recede like the tide. As thoughts and feelings return to the shores of your existence, use your breath and intention to guide them to gently float in your heart. Repose in this ethereal state of being.

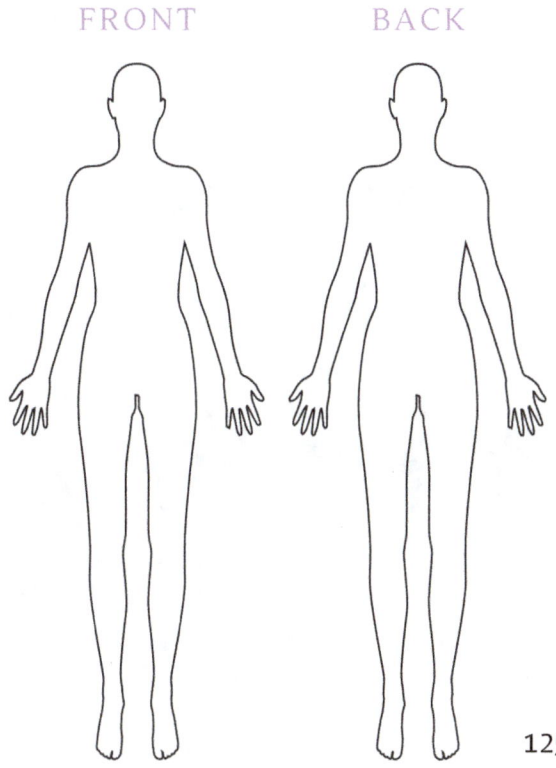

WHAT DO YOU NOTICE?

FRONT   BACK

125

93.

Feel no solid boundary
where your body ends or begins.
In this, find infinite form.

The smaller the ruler, the longer the coastline. The more finely you can measure, the less clear the boundary. Know this is true about yourself. Like the cosmos, your body is mostly empty space held together by electric and magnetic fields. The interior is constantly exchanging with its surroundings through breath, food, osmosis and as cells die and are replaced. The closer you look, the more unclear the distinction is where your form begins and ends.

What separates you from everything that is not "you", is your ever-glowing, ever-conscious center. Each being has its own contracted, individuated sense of presence. That centered self is not in the barrier of your skin, it is not on your edges. Like the sun, it is your radiating center that distinguishes you. The waves of your unique light move out into the world, blending with an endless ocean.

Understand yourself as infinite, regardless of your finite body. Feel yourself connected to all existence, tied together in this ocean of energy and consciousness. Linger with your infinite self and ponder your fuzzy edges.

WHAT DO YOU NOTICE?

FRONT   BACK

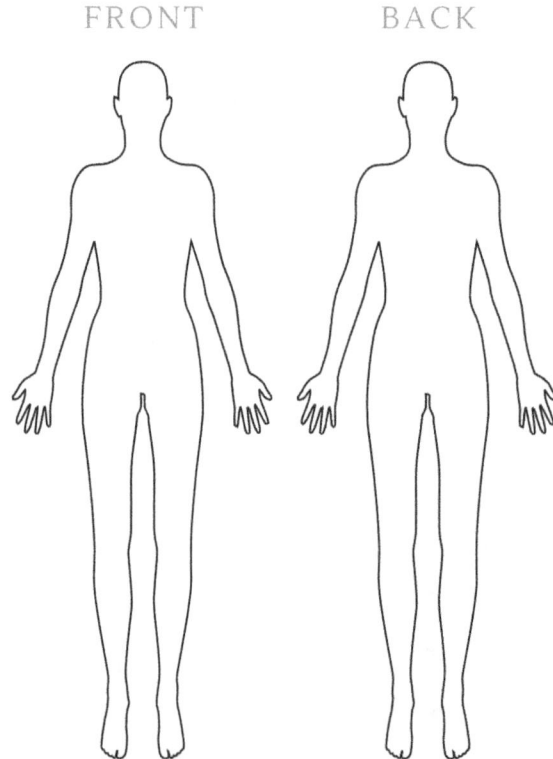

94. Feel yourself flooded with the same shining light that makes up the cosmos.

It is common to move through life feeling a hole in the heart and wounds in the soul. A person may try to fill the hole and heal the wounds with alcohol, sex, drugs, gambling, or any number of material things, only to find that the hole remains. The spiritual homesickness persists.

This meditation is an invitation to infuse these wounds in your soul with the energies of pure love and pure medicine that flow infinitely from the fabric of the universe. Understand that this is the same energy of creation that formed the cosmos and lead to your birth.

Close your eyes, inhale deeply, and let out a long sigh. Focus your mind and imagine what it looks like to be flooded with shining light that expands in you with each breath. Whatever you visualize is what you need, so receive this love into all your sore spots. As a child of the universe you are always worthy of receiving the ever-loving light that brought you into existence, even now.

WHAT DO YOU NOTICE?

FRONT   BACK

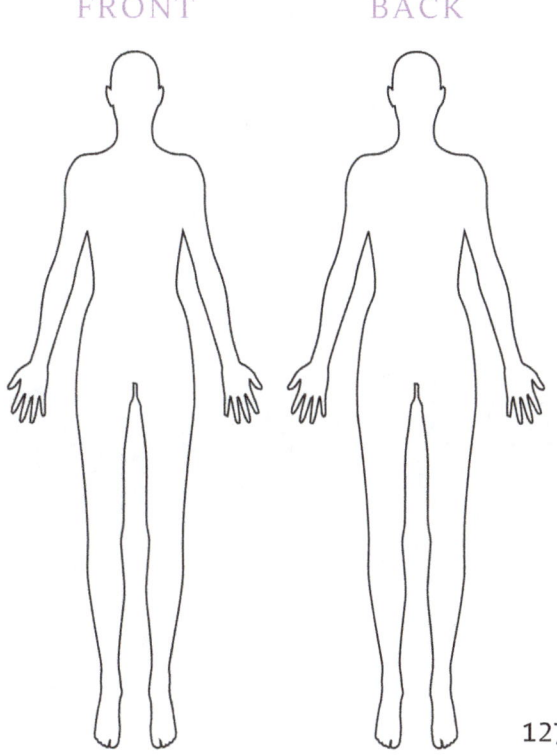

127

95.

Become aware of the subtle and vibrant
sensations of the body's sexual centers.

Embark on an intentional exploration of the subtle energy flows in your body. With no sexual desire in mind, gently direct your awareness to the breasts, the clitoris, and/or the tip of the lingham. Allow your presence and deep breath to guide this exploration without any goal, only curioisity.

Notice how the slightest touch or attention awakens a divine spark of electricity. Turn toward the stories that arise in your mind and meet them with love as you exhale back into presence. Remember, sexuality is like a flower, for each sensation unfolds in your body at its own pace like a petal in the spring. Again, breathe deeply and notice how you can expand and even move this sacred warmth throughout your body.

Through this sensory journey, learn how these sacred centers and their rippling sensations are a direct link to the same creative energy that made all existence. Treat this sensuality with the utmost reverence, for its power can be equally destructive when misused. Instead, hold it high, hold it with grace, and evolve your understanding of the nature of reality through the wisdom of your body.

WHAT DO YOU NOTICE?

FRONT   BACK

96.

Go somewhere you can see
for miles without interruption.
Feel that same clarity in your interior.

Open plains, treetops, mountaintops, skyscrapers, wide beaches, and rolling hills can all offer this view. If none of these are near you, it will be worth your while to take an adventure to go find one. Each of these perspectives share one thing. They remind you how small you are compared to the scale of the world.

Looking out over miles you may see tiny cars, tiny homes, and tiny people off in the distance. From high up, you can watch them move, each life a part of a much bigger system. A building that seems massive when you stand beneath it will shrink as your perspective grows. Even your daily life feels smaller to carry from up high.

This practice teaches you to zoom out, to step out of the stories of your life, and to give your mind a place of respite to do the same. Notice the foggy situations that suddenly become clear. Notice an ability to look down your own life's path for miles without interruption. And piercing through that space, notice something deeper.

WHAT DO YOU NOTICE?

FRONT   BACK

97. Imagine a vast field, the entire sky, or even just the entire room filled with your peaceful conscious self.

To begin, take a moment and take a breath to drop into your peaceful, awakened self. The natural serenity that comes from deep breathing and presence is akin to heat from a flame. It is one power that each person carries- if you can find pure presence then you can find a sense of peace.

Allow this serene, slow breathing self to fill your whole body. With each exhale it grows to embrace you, relaxing your muscles and heart. Continue expanding this peaceful field until it reaches beyond your physical body. What color, shape, and texture do you visualize? Whatever you see is a perfect representation of your bliss.

The more presence you offer, the more peace you have. Fill the room, fill the building with your love. Then go outside and use this practice to fill a whole valley, a whole field, a whole city, and even the whole sky with your peaceful conscious self. When you have done this, awaken to your true nature.

WHAT DO YOU NOTICE?

FRONT   BACK

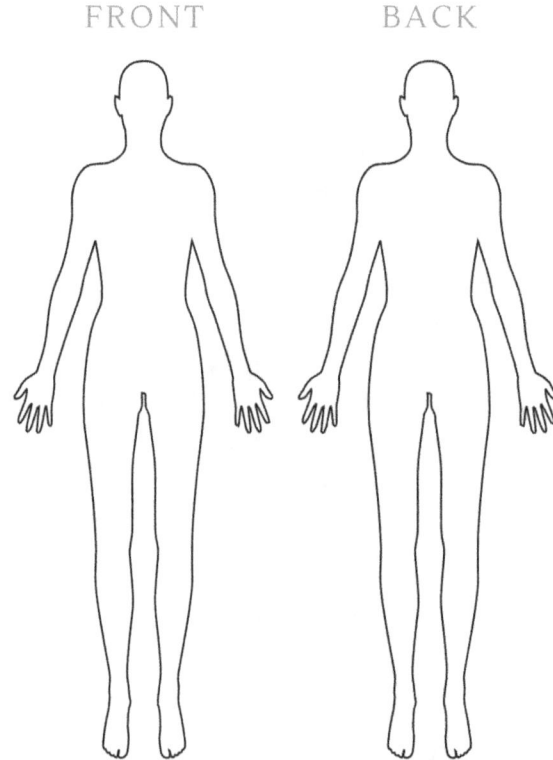

130

98. Offer gentle, soothing kindness to your heart. Be present to the peace that follows.

Using pressure waves and neurons, the heart is constantly sending felt messages to the rest of the body. Often these messages feel challenging or inconvenient so the natural tendency is to control or withhold its whims or yearnings.

It is natural to mistrust the heart when it conflicts with your mind's sense of logic. You may think you can't listen to your own heart because it once led you down a path that brought pain. You may try to ignore your heart when it is so sad that all life feels gray.

But what happens if you meet each one of those messages with gentle, soothing, kindness? Listen to your heart in all its joy and sorrow. Even when your mind and your gut tell you otherwise, let your heart's whispers at least be fully seen and heard. That doesn't mean to always act on them. Rather, be the understanding, nurturing caretaker that your heart has always needed and notice how it softens your whole being.

WHAT DO YOU NOTICE?

FRONT   BACK

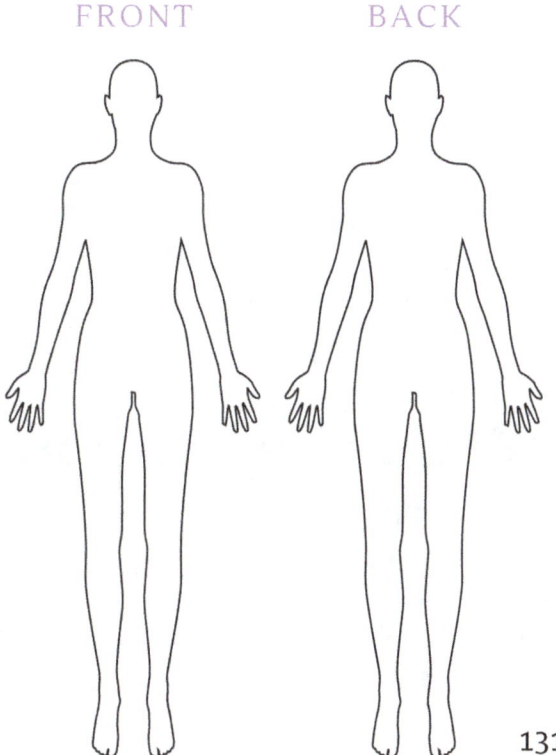

131

99. Use your willpower to expand your personal electromagnetic field in all directions.

As a living being, your body is constantly creating, emitting, and responding to electricity and magnetism. Your heart beats, your nervous system sings to itself, and your brain is in a perpetual lightning storm.

Each person feels these complex flows of energy in their own unique way. Some are like a leaf in the wind while others are completely unaware that such subtle energy exists. Those who are most at peace are riding the wave of each moment, using breath and intention to soothe and regulate their electromagnetic body.

When you find this balance point in yourself, use your breath and sacred imagination to envision expanding your energetic field in all directions. Send it up, send it down. Breathe it out to the east, south, west, and north. Do this practice and discover how big you can truly become. Discover that your capacity is so much greater than you thought.

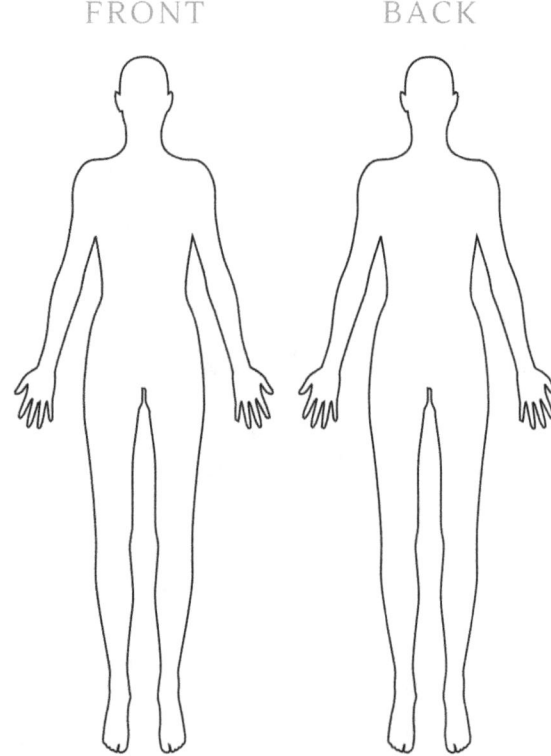

WHAT DO YOU NOTICE?

FRONT   BACK

There is a common misconception that enlightenment is the destination at the end of a person's spiritual journey. That when you arrive, you are so connected and peaceful that all your human suffering will end. In reality, enlightenment is a state of ever-loving, ever-present conscious awareness that is beyond all illusions and beyond all stories.

You may have had such an exalted experience or even more than one. The idea of spiritual practice is to give yourself a roadmap back to a state of enlightenment so that you can always find your way home anytime you need it, instead of once or twice in a lifetime.

The world will continue to have pain, frustration, loss, and discomfort. There will always be someone to challenge or trigger you. The body will still age and the mind will still wander. What changes is how quickly you find your way back home to total acceptance and peaceful awareness.

WHAT DO YOU NOTICE?

FRONT   BACK

101. Summon your limitless ability to learn and act, discovering your true powerful self.

The human mind has a fascinating ability to learn and grow throughout its entire lifespan. In most cases, the biggest limitation is a belief system which is internalized so deeply that a person may not feel worthy of achieving goals that are perfectly within their reach. On the other hand, there is no shortage of people who defy perceived limitations and put in the work to learn a new skill and succeed in an area where the world said they would fail.

Tantra teaches that everyone is capable of stepping beyond these limiting beliefs. This technique taps into each person's divine powers of willing, knowing, and acting. First, get centered and find your inspiration, then if you need to, gain knowledge to help you accomplish your goal. When you have knowledge, take the leap and act on your dream.

Think of something you always wanted to learn, but never pursued. Have you always wanted to paint, but never tried? Did you avoid chemistry because you're bad at math? Take a class and try again with a new perspective and faith in your brain. You can never be good at something unless you're willing to be bad at it first. Start learning and uncover the sacred birthright of your vast potential.

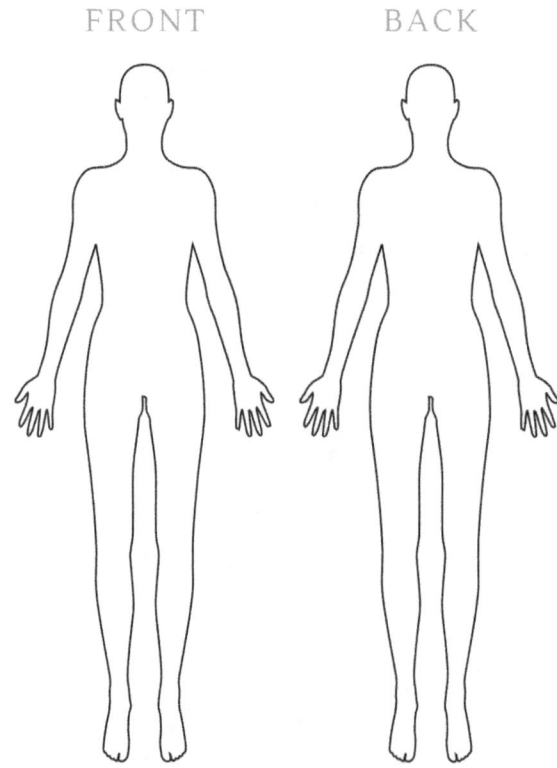

WHAT DO YOU NOTICE?

FRONT   BACK

102.

Feel consciousness dwelling in you and
all around you until you see it as all pervading.

Consciousness, is-ness, presence, awareness, that which perceives, that which experiences. Find that part of yourself in your body. Is it centrally located somewhere within you or is each part of you experiencing its own consciousness? What does your brain perceive? What does your microbiome experience? A mitochondria? Feel conscious awareness on all levels of your being.

Now look around you. Consider the consciousness of a plant that reaches towards the light. Witness the animals around you and observe their unique perception and interaction with the world. Witness their version of hunger, their fear, their contentment, and their sleep.

What of a stone? A table? Does each collection of particles have its own sense of an existence? Consider deeply what it would feel like to be a boulder. Engage in this wonderment until you experience consciousness to be as ever-present as we perceive space and time.

WHAT DO YOU NOTICE?

FRONT   BACK

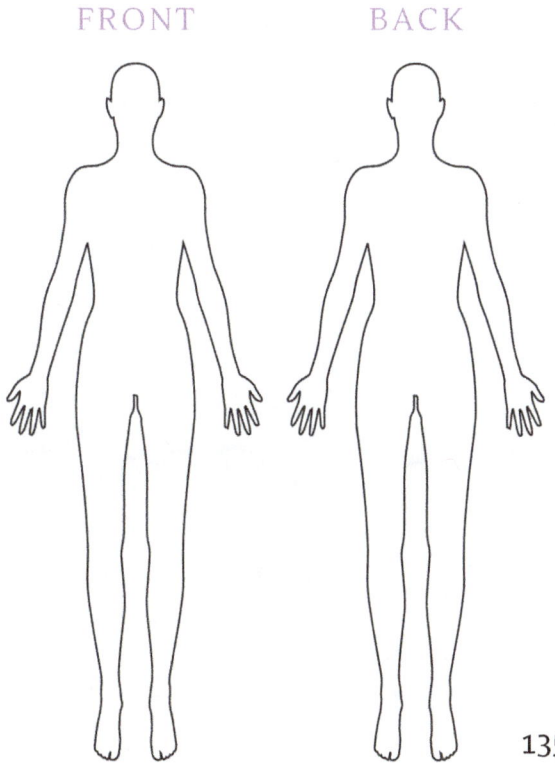

103. Meet each desire with total presence and clarity, not resistance.

Consider and understand life's equal and opposite reactions. That which you resist will persist. This is not to suggest that you give into your desires. Instead, open up a dialogue with the yearning to truly comprehend the desire and therefore yourself.

Whatever the desire, even if just for a sip of water, stop for a moment to become fully conscious of that urge. Wake yourself up from autopilot. Ask yourself if the thing you desire will support your highest and greatest good. Does it help you? Does it hurt others?

Tantra asks its practitioners to dive into these nuances. It doesn't forbid your desires, it asks you to develop your own sense of discernment and to learn what it means to have integrity. When you discover how it feels to have a clean, clear, and compassionate heart, then you will be able to meet each desire with total presence and discern what it is you really need.

WHAT DO YOU NOTICE?

FRONT   BACK

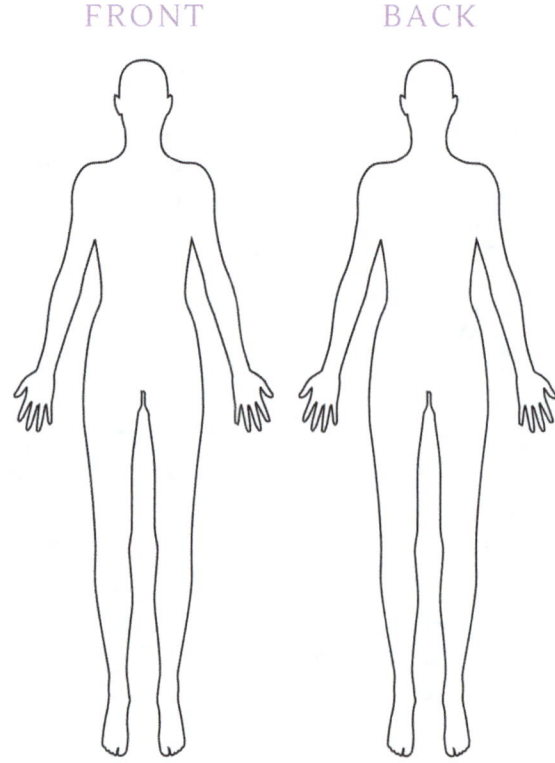

Focus your eyes and gaze at the farthest point you can see. Listen for the most distant sounds you can hear. What is the most subtle flavor on your tongue or the faintest scent in your nose? Let your awareness wander slowly and intentionally around these edges of your perception. When you find that boundary, linger there, see if you can reach just a little beyond.

Keep stretching your perception a little further with each breath until your mind's eye can envision what lies just past the edge. What is on the next mountain further than what you see? What can you hear that is beyond your hearing? What can you taste that is not in your mouth? What can you feel that is not currently touching your skin?

Melt into this exercise with your whole being and find that there is no limit to what you can perceive. There is no limit to where your conscious perception can take you.

WHAT DO YOU NOTICE?

FRONT   BACK

137

105. Open your mind to all existence as one vibrating, dancing field of consciousness and energy.

The tantric understanding of the nature of reality is that there is an expansive, undulating, glowing oneness that contains the potential for all existence. The first and most fundamental split in that oneness is into pure consciousness, or Shiva, and pure energy, or Shakti.

The interplay and dance of energy and consciousness sparked all the rest of existence as we know it, unfolding in layers of reality called tattvas. Observe and you can see a universe in constant motion all around you. The spark of an idea, the birth of a baby, a song being written, love, war- all it of it rising and falling in waves that weave and interact. A dancing field that is vibrating in an ever evolving, always balanced, expression of pure creativity on a cosmic scale.

This practice invites you to zoom all the way out from the scale of daily life to remember this cosmic choreography that created you and continues to embrace you in each moving moment.

WHAT DO YOU NOTICE?

FRONT   BACK

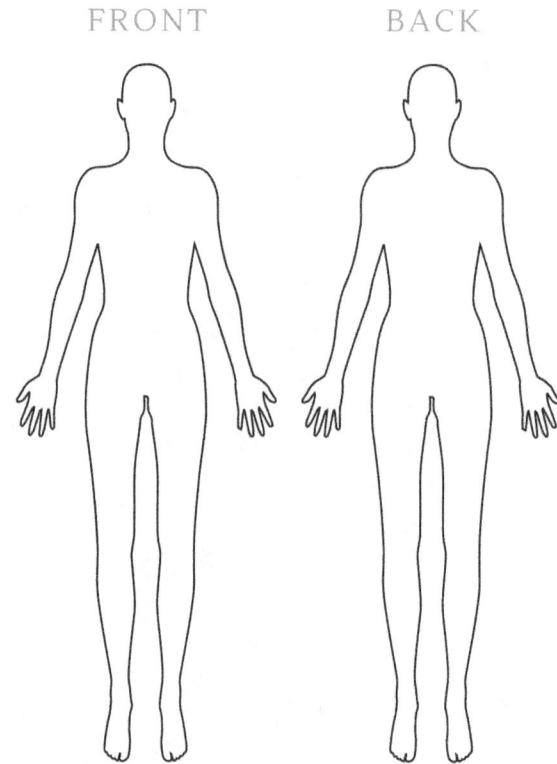

106.

Deeply imagine what it is like to exist as each being.
Experience each unique consciousness as your own.

Each being has a unique experience of existence. Tantra suggests that any thing that exists perceives you as you perceive it. Quantum physics refers to this as the observer effect- the presence of a human observer will effect the subject and the outcome of an experiment.

Allow this foundation to lead you on an exploration through the many experiences of conscious awareness. Use your breath, your focus, and your sacred imagination to embody each being. What would your world be like if you were in the body and the mind of an ant? More than just size, feel the bodily sensation of having six legs, the exciting perception of strong scent.

What is it to exist as a hundred year old oak tree? How does it feel to have your roots deeply planted beneath branches and leaves that reach to the sky? Let yourself wander the world with this technique. Connect and learn from each animal, each plant, each person, each stone. Witness each being and discover the wisdom in each one.

WHAT DO YOU NOTICE?

FRONT   BACK

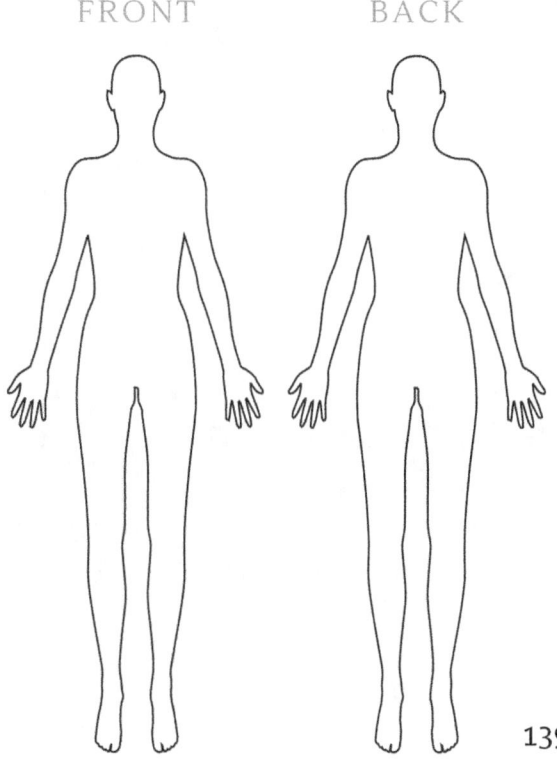

139

107. Contemplate consciousness as the only thing that truly exists.

What if consciousness is as essential to reality as we perceive space and time to be? What if a glacier, absent all human language, is having a slow, dense, passive, observing experience beyond human time?

Indeed, what if sentience itself underpins it all? In a tantric worldview, time and space only exist because they are being perceived. This technique asks you to suspend your disbelief and sit with this paradoxical abstraction.

Consider all reality as an ocean of consciousness that creates the world we know by forming bubbles of individuated sentience that have forgotten their true nature so that consciousness can more fully experience the world it created.

What if your whole spiritual journey is a process of following clues that lead you back to the ocean that created you? What if enlightenment is shedding your bubble of forgetfulness and dissolving back into your true nature of oneness, of pure consciousness?

WHAT DO YOU NOTICE?

FRONT   BACK

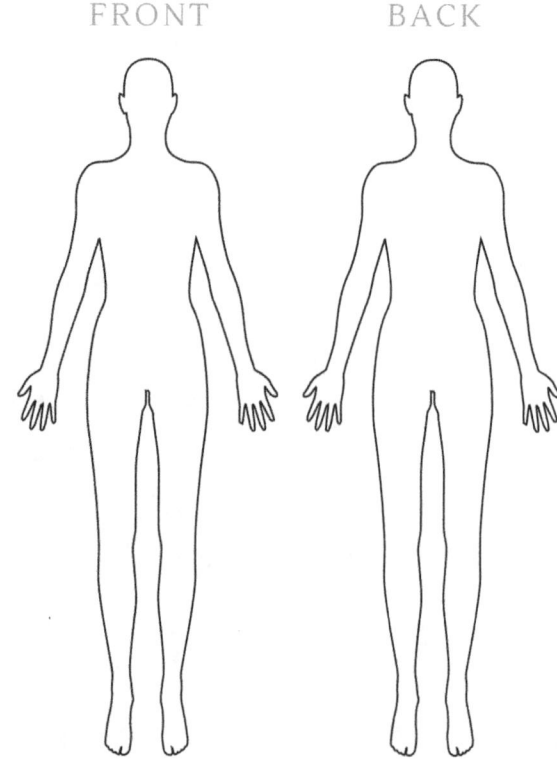

108.

Learn to be your own teacher, guide, guru, and the expert of your own inner world.

Classical Tantra describes three pillars to a strong spiritual practice- a teacher, sacred texts, and personal experience. Without one of the three, you run the risk of following a wayward path and slipping into a spiritual pitfall.

Each of these pillars is an avenue to validate spiritual truths. A teacher and a student can both be lead astray without a lineage of texts to ground their studies. The same can happen with a student using personal experience and texts alone. And, of course, teachings and a teacher mean nothing when they aren't connected to your personal experience.

Whichever teachers and texts you use, let your personal experience guide you to connect with them and to know yourself so deeply that you fully embody the spiritual truths they contain. Not to negate your other teachers, but to trust yourself to stand amongst them. Let the wisdom come alive in you until you evolve into your own inner guide, lovingly navigating each moment of reality with grace and ease.

WHAT DO YOU NOTICE?

FRONT   BACK

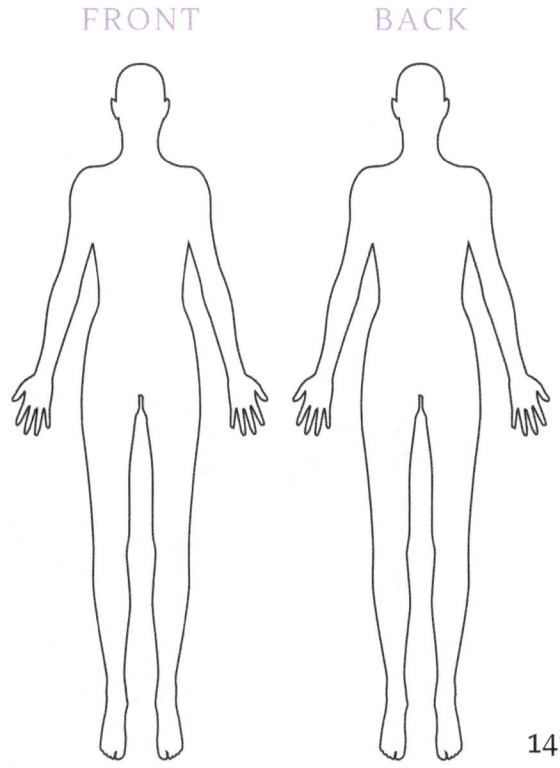

141

109. Imagine the interior of your body as empty, simply defined by a sheath of skin.

Dive into an imaginative exploration of your body with this technique. Have you ever seen inside your body? What if it is as hollow as a cave? Try to visualize the thin layer of skin that separates you from the world around you.

Breathe deeply, focus, and imagine a clear vacant cavern running from your finger tips, to your head, to your toes. Imagine a ball could bounce from wall to wall within you. Connect deeply with this vision of your body as an empty void, full of space and beyond time. What if each big inhale filled you like a balloon from head to toe?

Can you float here in this realm of timeless time and spaceless space? Understand that this conscious, quiet void is a path to your true nature that is free of the burdens of human experience. Bring the serene stillness of your inner void to each waking moment and find bliss.

WHAT DO YOU NOTICE?

FRONT   BACK

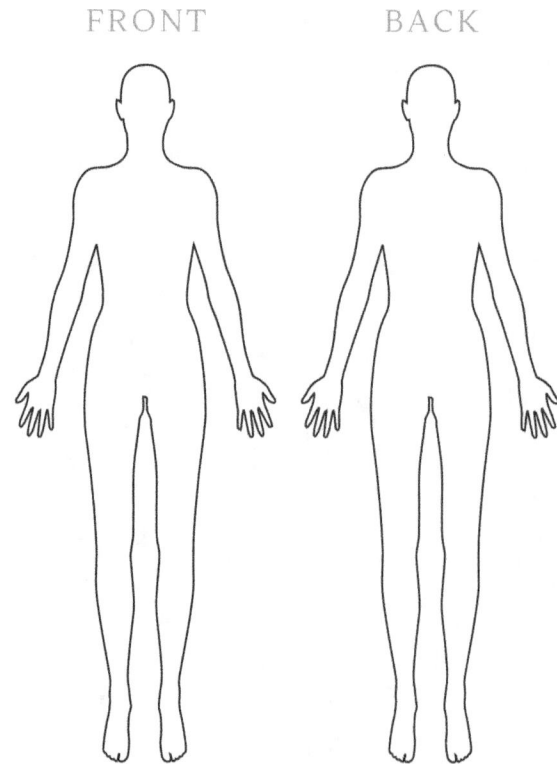

110.
Like the Divine itself,
be playful and curious in life.

The world can be such a heavy place and the people in it even heavier. It is easy to get lost in life's painful, hard stories because they do exist, they are real. From millennia of being hunted by predators, the human brain even has a bias towards remembering and focusing on potential threats and pain.

Sometimes it is important to immerse yourself in that heaviness and learn the lessons it has to teach you. But it is equally important to remember that light is what creates shadows, it is always there. There is always room and opportunity to cross back from darkness to light, from pain to joy.

Divine consciousness is naturally curious and playful in its journey to experience all things. Creation just for the sake of creation. Try it- practice random acts of kindness and senseless acts of beauty. Go discover something new to you. Meet shadow like a jigsaw puzzle on a winter day. Hold all of life lightly like its a game you love to play.

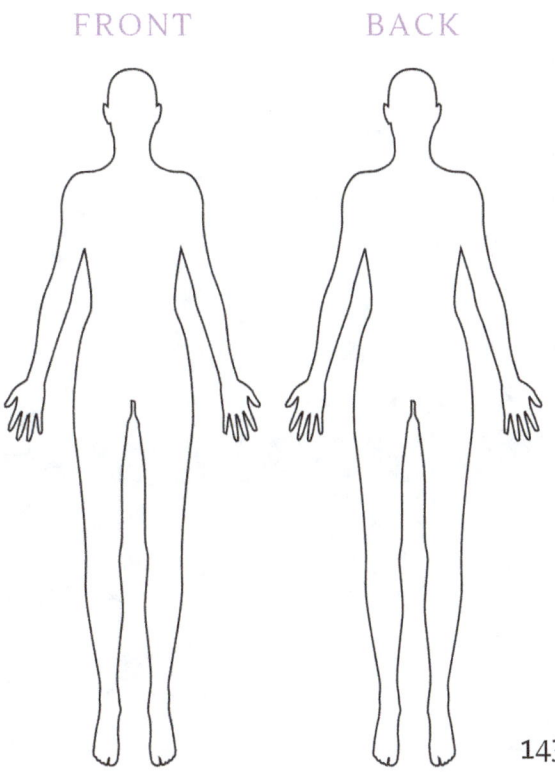

WHAT DO YOU NOTICE?

FRONT   BACK

Consider good vs bad,
knowledge vs ignorance, inner vs outer.
Then go beyond to a perspective that includes all.

Dualistic thinking is a natural consequence of being born into the human experience. The choice of either this or that begins as soon as you come out of the womb and are labeled as either a girl or a boy, whether or not it fits. It continues as you grow and adults label you as smart or slow, good or bad, talented or not.

Consider all the things that you view in a dualistic way. Be honest with yourself as you reflect. Can a criminal still be a good person? Can you feel both sorrow and joy? Can night and day intermingle? Know this as a fundamental truth about our world. Even subatomic particles have a weird way of blinking in and out of existence and showing up in more than one place at the same time.

Stretch your ability to coexist with and embrace contradicting truths. Transcend bondage and liberation, knowing and not knowing, existing and not existing. Embrace both and let go completely. In this, find yourself more fluid, more open, and more wise. In this, find your whole, nondual self.

WHAT DO YOU NOTICE?

FRONT   BACK

112.

Bring your awareness
to the quiet, vast
space within.

The tantric worldview sees the human body as a microcosm of the whole universe. All its light, all its shadow, and all that lies in between are contained within you. Everything that you could ever need or want exists in some form in your inner world. You just have to journey to find it.

Be not afraid of your shadows because you also contain the brightest light, the ever-glowing warmth of pure consciousness. Let that light shine love, acceptance, and healing on all that you find in yourself. Remember that only light can overcome shadow.

Breathe deeply and allow your focus to dig deeper and discover your sacred self. Love your pain, love your shame, love your anger, and uncover the beauty that lives in those dark corners. Let the light of your awareness soften your hard edges and illuminate each vast cavern of your being. In all of your messy glory you will find the true nature of reality. The macrocosm will reveal itself to you when you dance in your own spaceless space.

WHAT DO YOU NOTICE?

FRONT   BACK

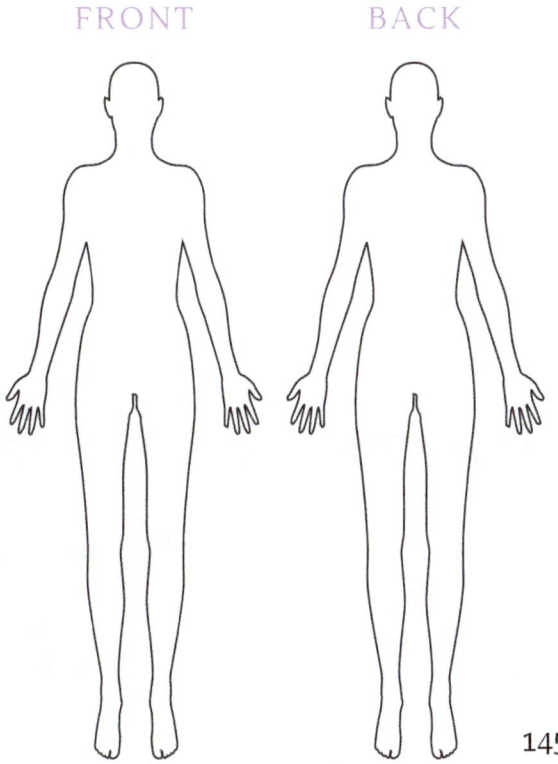